I Am Jesus: *Let's Change the World*

I Am Jesus

Let's Change the World

MY **EXCEPTIONAL** FOLLOWERS

MAKE AN **EXPONENTIAL** CHURCH

ELMER L. TOWNS

DESTINY IMAGE® PUBLISHERS, INC.
P.O. Box 310, Shippensburg, PA 17257-0310
"Promoting Inspired Lives."

This book and all other Destiny Image and Destiny Image Fiction books are available at Christian bookstores and distributors worldwide.

For more information on foreign distributors, call 717-532-3040.
Or reach us on the Internet: www.destinyimage.com

Cover and Interior Design by
Rob Williams, InsideOut Creative Arts
insideoutcreativearts.com

ISBN 13: TP 978-0-7684-4986-0
ISBN 13 EBook: 978-0-7684-4987-7
For Worldwide Distribution, Printed in the U.S.A.
1 2 3 4 5 6 7 8 9 10 11 / 22 21 20 19 18

CONTENTS

PART ONE

I AM JESUS: LET'S CHANGE THE WORLD

PART TWO

LET'S TALK: 50 DAILY DEVOTIONALS

INTRODUCTION

I am Jesus—the Church. The Bible identified the church as My body, "The church is his body; it is made full and complete by Christ" (Eph. 1:23, *NLT*). I am the Church made up of My followers, "Where two or three gather together as my followers, I am there among them" (Matt. 18:20, *NLT*). So, how do I grow since I am Jesus? The church ought to grow as I did as a young boy: "Jesus grew in wisdom and in stature and in favor with God and all the people" (Luke 2:52, *NLT*).

As a boy I grew in four areas: (1) intellectual ability, (2) physical measurement, (3) spiritually before the Father, and (4) socially according to the expectations of all the people.

Therefore, My local churches ought to grow in these same four areas. First, my local church must grow in knowledge of the Scriptures, doctrinal understanding and wisdom of divine growth principles, i.e., exponential growth (that growing according to the formula of the Great Commission).

Second, My church should grow in stature, through observable measures of baptisms, of members, of attendance, of offerings, and people involved in ministry.

Third, My church should grow in faith with the heavenly Father; this is spiritual growth—that means individual growth in prayer and fasting, with growth of corporate prayer and fasting. Also, members should individually grow spiritually. The local body should grow more spiritual in all their outward relationships and duties. All should seek fellowship with Me, intimacy with one another, and all should worship both the Father and Me (John 4:23, 24).

Finally, My local body should grow socially with the community as they serve the needs of both individuals and the neighborhoods where they live.

Just as I grew from a tiny infant into full manhood, My local body must grow exponentially into a full local church body that glorifies the Father in heaven and has a good testimony with all outside the church.

FOREWORD

I AM JESUS: LET'S CHANGE THE WORLD

I am Jesus who comes to live in your life at salvation. In this book you will learn the importance of becoming My exceptional follower so that you fellowship together with others in an exponential church. The Father in heaven sent Me to be born of a virgin—without sin. I lived a perfect life—without sin. Even though satan tempted Me to obey him and reject who I was, I didn't sin; I won that victory over him. On the cross I died for the sins of the world—your sins. I won the victory for all who will put their faith in Me; I give them eternal life. Now I want you to grow in your faith to become an exceptional follower who reaches out to the lost.

AN EXCEPTIONAL FOLLOWER

An exceptional Christian is one who grows to love Me with "all their heart, soul and mind" (Matt. 22:37, *NLT*). The word *exceptional* means extraordinary, or remarkable, or unexpected. I want you to be transformed and live for greater goals (Phil. 3:10-14), to be motivated with greater desires (Phil. 4:14), and let the gospel light shine through you to others (Phil. 2:16). I want you to be exceptional in your life and service.

AN EXPONENTIAL CHURCH

When you come together with other Christians, I am there: "For where two or three gather together as my followers, I am there among them" (Matt. 18:20, *NLT*). That gathering is also called My body (Eph. 1:22-23). So when you see an assembly (the Greek word *church* means assembly), you are looking at Me and you can see My influence through them. The main task of a church is the Great Commission, "Go into all the world and preach the Good News to everyone" (Mark 16:15, *NLT*). That is your task.

Exponential means rapid increase in all areas according to a predetermined formula. The Great Commission was the predetermined formula, the Holy Spirit was the source of increase, and the result was Me—a living, growing body efficient in ministry that exhibits all the strengths that a church was predicted to become.

Notice that the 7 chapters in this book all have to do with exceptional followers making an exponential church.

EXCEPTIONAL BELIEVERS MAKE MY CHURCH EXPONENTIAL

50 DAYS OF DEVOTIONS

I died on the cross on the Jewish Passover, and I arose on the third day. During the next 50 days I was equipping My disciples to carry out the Great Commission. I want to equip you and members in your church to do the same thing. After 50 days of waiting and praying, the Holy Spirit came upon the church on the day of Pentecost (Pentecost means fifty). Immediately, My church began winning people with the gospel, so much so that the enemy accused it of "turning the world upside down" (Acts 17:6).

Now I want to talk to you in 50 daily devotionals that are included at the end of this book. These devotionals will challenge you to an exponential ministry of outreach.

Then there are daily prayers so that you can talk to Me. You will pray for a burden for lost people and a vision of what I can do in your life and through your church. You will pray for your leaders, fellow workers, and the total outreach of your church. It will be an exciting 50 days—if you and your people ask for a great victory.

PART ONE

I Am
Jesus

Let's Change the World

I AM JESUS:

A Church Growing Exponentially

> *"He makes the whole body fit together perfectly. As each part*
> *does its own special work, it helps the other parts grow, so that*
> *the whole body is healthy and growing and full of love."*
>
> EPHESIANS 4:16, *NLT*

Because I, Jesus, gave the commission to preach the Gospel to every person, the exponential church aggressively carried out My command. Because I promised to give whatsoever asked in My name, a growing church fulfilled My promise. Because I promised "anyone who believes in me will do the same works I have done, and even greater works" (John 14:12, *NLT*), an evangelistic church became a reality. Because the exponential church saturates its area with the gospel, going everywhere to "turn the world upside down" (Acts 17:6), it becomes a greater challenge for all churches to be *exponential* in all they are and to reach the world for Christ.

Exponential means rapid increase in all areas according to a predetermined formula. The Great Commission was that formula, the Holy Spirit was the source of increase, and the result was a rapidly growing congregation efficient in all ministry that exhibits all that Christianity was predicted to become.

EXPONENTIAL EVANGELISM

The early church practiced *exponential evangelism*, filling Jerusalem with the gospel. Their enemies accused them, "Did we not strictly command you not to teach in this name? And look, you have filled Jerusalem with your doctrine" (Acts 5:28, *NKJV*). They filled their Jerusalem with the gospel, so must you. Your "Jerusalem" is that area the Holy Spirit has laid upon your heart. Those are the people you must saturate with the gospel. Sometimes your Jerusalem will be larger than the immediate neighborhood around your church. To some, your Jerusalem is your county; to others your Jerusalem is your state. Then others will have a Jerusalem that is greater than one state; it may be many states or nations.

How can you fill your "Jerusalem" with the gospel? The following definition was used by Jerry Falwell to describe how he got the job done: "Preaching the gospel to every available person, by every available means, at every available time."[1]

EXPONENTIAL VISION

Jerry Falwell first came to Lynchburg, Virginia, to start Thomas Road Baptist Church. He eventually built the 9th largest church in America. His vision was the secret of God's success through him. He posted a map on the back wall of his small church auditorium and drew a circle representing one mile in circumference around the church. He determined to visit every single home within that one-mile area. Beginning at 9:00 AM each morning, and working late into the evening, he visited every home with the purpose of (1) inviting them to church, (2) leaving a testimony of Christ, (3) offering to help them spiritually, and (4) when possible, attempting to lead someone to Jesus Christ. When he finished the first one-mile circumference, he extended his circle to two miles, then three miles, and before long, the circle included the whole city of Lynchburg, and then the surrounding counties. Then through television and radio, he extended his Jerusalem to the state of Virginia; next the United States, and then the world. His Jerusalem began with Lynchburg but eventually encompassed the world. Why did his congregation work so hard with him? One of the first laws of leadership states, "When followers buy into your vision, they will follow your leadership." You must pray for the Father to give you an *exponential vision* for your Jerusalem. As I help you evangelize your Jerusalem, your church can grow just as large as your vision.

EXPONENTIAL PRAYING

Originally, there were 120 people in the Upper Room praying for power to fulfill the Great Commission: "Peter stood up in the midst of the disciples, and said, (the number of names together were about a hundred and twenty)" (Acts 1:15). The early church grew because of *exponential praying*. Just praying is not enough to saturate your Jerusalem with the gospel; you must use *exponential* praying. What was this? In the church in Jerusalem, "They were all praying" (Acts 2:1), "They were all in one accord" (Acts 2:1), "They were all in one place" (Act 2:1), and "They were all filled with the Holy Spirit" (Acts 2:4). *Exponential vision* leads to *exponential prayer* that will result in *exponential evangelism*. That means (1) getting everyone to pray for spiritual power, (2) getting everyone to come together for prayer, and (3) getting focused prayer for evangelism. Also remember all the disciples were praying, all the men were praying, and all the women were praying.

EXPONENTIAL GROWTH

Peter preached a very simple sermon on the day of Pentecost, a sermon that can be read in less than four minutes. As a result, "They that gladly received his word were baptized: and the same day there were added unto them about three thousand souls" (Acts 2:41). In one day the church jumped from 120 people to over 3,000 people. That's *exponential growth*.

The next numerical indication of growth in the Jerusalem church was, "Howbeit many of them which heard the word believed; and the number of the men was about five thousand" (Acts 4:4). Now this is not just 5,000 Christians. The Greek word for "men" is not mankind, but males. The new converts represented 5,000 heads of households. Just as the men who were heads of households were counted in the book of Numbers, so the Jerusalem Church made up of mostly Jews counted the same way. So, with 5,000 men, there were 5,000 wives, and probably 2 to 4 children per family; so, there was a church of 20-30,000 converts. That's *exponential blessing*.

Next, the church had *exponential expansion*. So many were being saved that they no longer counted with exact numeric numbers, "And believers were the more added to the Lord, multitudes both of men and women" (Acts 5:14). Instead of using exact figures to measure this new growing church, they described it as a "multitude." When you have *exponential expansion*, it means both men and women. Why did they stop posting attendance figures? Because there were so many new converts in this church, they couldn't count them. Like massive demonstrations when multitudes gather, there were so many—they just couldn't count them.

EXPONENTIAL TEACHING

Next, there was *exponential teaching*. Notice what the 3,120 new converts did: "They continued steadfastly in the apostles' doctrine" (Acts 2:42) (the word *doctrine* in the *King James* is the verb for teaching, as seen in another modern versions), and "All the believers devoted themselves to the apostles' teaching" (Acts 2:42, *NLT*). If you want to have an *exponential church*, you must have *exponential teaching* of the Word of God. How is that done? (1) You must continue teaching as the Jerusalem church did, which means every day individuals were studying scripture, every day at the family altar, every Sunday in the church, i.e., all times with all methods. (2) You must teach the whole Bible from Genesis 1:1 to Revelation 22:21. (3) Next, you must teach the Scriptures "steadfastly," which means you teach with confidence and with purpose. Then you are *exponentially teaching* the Bible, which means you are confident that it is the inspired Word of God that will transform lives. *Exponential teaching* is instructing even if no other church teaches and instructing when you don't want to teach.

EXPONENTIAL FELLOWSHIP

Next, the early church had *exponential fellowship*. This does not mean drinking a lot of coffee or eating a lot of donuts together. No! See how *exponential fellowship* was practiced in the early church, "And all that believed were together" (Acts 2:44). It means they all attended services at the same time. You can't have an *exponential church* if some members are absent and other members are not regular in attendance. When some members choose not to attend worship services, they reflect a lack of spirituality. The early church was a gathered church, "And they, continuing daily with one accord in the temple, and breaking bread from house to house" (Acts 2:46). *Exponential fellowship* means Christians coming together on a face-to-face basis in (1) regular attendance, (2) making church worship a priority over personal pursuits, (3) attending church to obey God's Word, and (4) using their spiritual gifts in service through the church. *Exponential fellowship* means desiring to fellowship with your church to do everything I want you to do when Christians meet together.

EXPONENTIAL WORSHIP

Because I was in the midst of the church, they had *exponential worship*. What were Christians doing? "Praising God" (Acts 2:47). I had told the Samaritan woman, "The Father seeks worshippers" (John

4:23, *NLT*). Because the Father wants My people to worship Him, an *exponential church* has *exponential worship*. Worship is defined as "giving God the worthship that is due to Him." When you *exponentially praise* the Father, you pour out your appreciation to Him. When you *exponentially exalt* the Father, you put Him at the pinnacle of your life. When you *exponentially magnify* the Father, you give Him the "largest" place in your life. When you *exponentially worship* the Father, you give Him everything in your life.

EXPONENTIAL BOLDNESS

The Jewish Sanhedrin threatened the Christians in Jerusalem against speaking in My name, but Christians continued witnessing and sharing the gospel. They didn't stop ministering because of their opposition. When threatened, the entire church went to prayer: "Lord, behold their threatenings: and grant unto thy servants, that with all boldness they may speak thy word" (Acts 4:29).

How did I respond to their prayers? "When they had prayed, the place was shaken where they were assembled together; and they were all filled with the Holy Spirit and spake the word of God with boldness" (Acts 4:31). Again, this is *exponential praying*. This was not the average prayer I hear, "... if it is Your will." They prayed for boldness and I gave them exponential boldness to evangelize their Jerusalem.

Exponential praying results in *exponential boldness*. Because of their prayer meeting, "They spake the word of God with boldness" (Acts 4:31). *Exponential boldness* is witnessing to your close family members, your relatives, people you don't know, even testifying for Me to those who oppose you and object to what you say.

EXPONENTIAL PERSONAL EVANGELISM

Next, the church had *exponential personal evangelism*. The Bible says, "And daily in the temple, and in every house, they ceased not to teach and preach Jesus Christ" (Acts 5:42). *Exponential personal evangelism* is going house to house so no one misses the message. They were not just passing out tracts or church flyers. *Exponential personal evangelism* was "preaching and teaching Jesus Christ." In each home, Christians were explaining who I am and what I did on the cross.

Because of *exponential personal evangelism*, the church stepped up to a higher level of attainment, "When the number of the disciples was multiplied" (Acts 6:1). The Holy Spirit instituted a higher level of arithmetic. Previously the Holy Spirit added to My church; now He multiplies. Everyone knows the difference between adding and multiplying. If someone were to ask for money and you give them ten dollars and added another ten dollars, they might say, "Twenty dollars is not enough." Ten dollars multiplied by ten dollars is one hundred dollars. Multiplication compounds the results. That's what was happening to the church. So many people were getting saved, they were having *exponential multiplication*. What is *exponential multiplication*? When someone you win to Christ turns around to win someone else, you rejoice because they are your spiritual children and spiritual grandchildren.

EXPONENTIAL ORGANIZATION

Growth caused conflict in the early church. Some widows with Jewish names were getting bigger and better welfare than widows with Gentile names: "There arose a murmuring of the Grecians against the Hebrews, because their widows were neglected in the daily ministration" (Acts 6:1). Look what happened—*exponential organization*—this is a church continually organizing to continue evangelizing and ministering. Some churches have bureaucratic organization, which places emphasis on creating smooth-running committees and boards. But many times it is static and entrenched. Good organization always grows to accommodate winning souls and teaching My Word. A church should have *exponential organization* to continually carry out the Great Commission. Rick Warren's title for a church fits this theme, *A Purpose-Driven Church.*[2] A purpose-driven church is *exponentially organized* to continually carry out the Great Commission.

What happened when the church was properly organized? The disciples gave themselves "continually to prayer, and to the ministry of the word" (Acts 5:6:4).

The next thing about *exponential organization* is that it starts at the top and works its way down. The church chose workers who were "full of the Holy Spirit, full of wisdom" (Acts 6:3). The "brethren", which meant church membership, were to find seven men who fit the spiritual qualifications, but church leadership, i.e., the pastors, had the final say, "Whom we may appoint over this business" (Acts 6:3). They wanted to continue preaching and teaching Jesus Christ (Acts 5:42).

What was the result of *exponential organization?* "The word of God increased; and the number of the disciples multiplied in Jerusalem greatly" (Acts 6:7). Exponential organization resulted in *exponential multiplication*. Previously, the church was adding new members, "now believers were multiplied greatly" (Acts 6:7)

EXPONENTIAL CHURCH PLANTING

Next was *exponential church planting*: "The churches . . . were edified; and walking in the fear of the Lord, and in the comfort of the Holy Ghost, were multiplied" (Acts 9:31). Up until now, I have been describing one church growing, i.e., the Jerusalem church. Now, new churches are being planted, "The churches were multiplied." This means *exponential church planting*.

The gospel was taken to Antioch in Syria, a heathen city. How did the believers begin witnessing? "They preached the Word to none but the Jews, only" (Acts 11:19). But then they began to witness "unto the Grecians, preaching the LORD Jesus" (Acts 11:20). This is *exponential evangelism*. When the gospel is preached to Christians on Sunday, that is expected preaching. But when you preach to the unsaved or to the heathen, then that is exponential preaching. Witnessing to people of a different race, or those living in different cultures, that is *exponential evangelism*.

Notice what happened in Antioch: "And the hand of the Lord was with them: and a great number believed and turned unto the Lord" (Acts 11:21). Again, I emphasized a great number who became Christians. This happened because of *exponential evangelism*. When people are skeptical of the validity of your message, you can use numbers to convince them of your credibility. While numbers are not the final criteria, you can use numbers because I did.

EXPONENTIAL LEADERSHIP

The church in Antioch was growing because everyone was witnessing. Then things began to really happen when they got *exponential leadership*. The report of the growth of the Antioch church came to Jerusalem, and they sent Barnabas to help the young church. What do we know about Barnabas? "He was a good man, and full of the Holy Spirit and of faith" (Acts 11:24). We know that Barnabas defended Paul in Jerusalem when no one else did. Barnabas was an aggressive leader, but when he came to this Gentile church, he became an *exponential leader*. What happened? "Much people were added unto the Lord" (Acts 11:24).

EXPONENTIAL GIVING

The next problem to face the church was a famine in Jerusalem. In your terminology, it's like a recession or a depression. So Barnabas instituted a policy of *exponential giving*. He determined to gather a large financial collection to send and help the Christians in Jerusalem. What is *exponential giving*? "Every man according to his ability, determined to send relief unto the brethren which dwelt in Judaea" (Acts 11:29). *Exponential giving* is not everyone giving the same amount, but everyone giving according to their ability. The early church continued the practice of tithing, because each believer gives a tenth of his income. Both the rich and poor give according to their income. This is called proportional giving and it is fair to all. This is also called *exponential giving* because "everyone," that means all in the church, "gave." If you really believe the message of the Great Commission that all people are lost and need the gospel, and if you really believe that I commanded you to carry out the Great Commission, then you will become involved in *exponential giving* to provide resources so that all may hear the gospel.

EXPONENTIAL FASTING

The church at Antioch was praying and fasting, "As they ministered to the Lord, and fasted" (Acts 13:2). Their prayer and fasting were successful because "The Holy Ghost said, 'Separate me Barnabas and Saul for the work whereunto I have called them'" (Acts 13:2). Thus far, the gospel had gone out, but one thing was lacking. The church didn't have a strategy to carry the gospel into all the world. They got that strategy because of *exponential fasting*. When Christians fast, they move into the area of sacrificial living. When you fast from food, you give up that which you enjoy. Also, when you fast, you give that which is necessary, because all must eat to live. So, when you fast at a certain time—one day or ten days—you are fasting and praying for Me to fulfill a certain purpose. The church at Antioch was getting ready for an *exponential strategy* that grew out of *exponential fasting*.

What does *exponential fasting* do? (a) It enables you to hear the voice of God, just as the church in Antioch heard the Holy Spirit, (b) it enables you to sacrifice (God asked the church to give up its

leadership, i.e., Barnabas and Saul), and (c) *exponential fasting* resulted in world evangelism.

EXPONENTIAL PENETRATION

When Barnabas and Saul began their missionary journey, they
might have asked, "How are we to complete the work of God in a
strange land?" The Holy Spirit told them what to do: "When they
had gone through the isle unto Paphos" (Acts 13:6). This is *exponential penetration*. They went from one end of the island to the other.
They penetrated cities, homes, businesses and lives. That's what you
must do as a strategy; you must take the gospel to every person at
every geographical place, in every area of their life. That leads to
the last principle.

SUMMARY AND CONCLUSION

Exponential evangelism is described as "using every available means
(methods) to reach every available person at every available time."
That means when you are *exponentially* reaching your town for
Christ, you have saturated every area of living and you have saturated every life. When Barnabas and Saul went through the entire
island of Cyprus, they were fulfilling the natural desire of their heart;
they were using exponential saturation.

Chapter Two

I AM JESUS:
A Revived Church

"I will pour out My Spirit on all people."

JOEL 2:28, NLT

"And everyone present was filled with the Holy Spirit."

ACTS 2:4, NLT

When I ascended into heaven, the disciples returned to Jerusalem and met together with about one hundred and twenty people to pray. Things just didn't seem right without Me. While they knew something special was going to happen, there was a feeling that something was out of place. There were twelve tribes in Israel and I had called twelve apostles. But there were only eleven of them. Perhaps they feared their ministry would not emerge until "the eleven" once more became "the twelve."

Peter arose to remind them that the betrayal of Judas Iscariot was consistent with the prophecies that I, the Messiah, would be betrayed. Peter pointed out that the sin of Judas should not surprise them. Peter cited two psalms (Ps. 69:25; 109:8) as a basis to appoint a new twelfth disciple.

Several conditions were quickly established to appoint a disciple to replace Judas Iscariot. First, the new disciple would have travelled with Me from the beginning (after John the Baptist baptized Me).

Second, the new disciple should have been a witness of both My resurrection and ascension. Of those present, only two appeared to meet all these qualifications: Joseph Justus, who was also known as Barabbas, and Matthias.

With two equally qualified candidates for one office, the disciples were not prepared to make a decision themselves without divine guidance. Together they prayed, "You, O Lord, who know the hearts of all, show which of these two You have chosen to take part in this ministry and apostleship from which Judas by transgression fell" (Acts 1:24-25, *NKJV*). Then, relying upon the Old Testament custom of casting lots, they determined Matthias was the one who should serve in Judas Iscariot's place: "And he was numbered with the eleven disciples" (Acts 1:26, *NKJV*).

During the two weeks between My ascension and the Day of Pentecost, with times of searching, confession, worship and intercession, corporate prayer took place. By the end of the waiting period, a spirit of unity governed the group as "they were all with one accord in one place" (Acts 2:1, *NKJV*).

THE HOLY SPIRIT POURED OUT

Quite unexpectedly, a number of strange phenomena began to take place in the Upper Room. First, there was a sound of a strong gust of wind that echoed off the walls of the room, but no one was blown about. Then divided tongues that looked like flames of a fire fell on each of them, but no one was burned. Third, "they were all filled with the Holy Spirit" (Acts 2:4, *NKJV*), an experience that had previously happened on only rare occasions in the Old Testament, and almost never in a group setting. Each of them began to speak clearly in foreign languages they had never learned. All this happened very early on the Day of Pentecost, before 9:00 in the morning.

Because Jewish males were required by the Law of Moses to attend the feast of Passover (Deut. 16:16), the city was crowded with pious Jewish men from around the Roman Empire who had come to celebrate Pentecost. News of what had taken place in the Upper Room quickly spread through the crowded city. A crowd formed around the disciples, people were divided in their opinion of what was happening. At least sixteen different language groups heard these Galileans speaking fluently in their native tongue. Others, probably unable to understand the different languages, simply assumed the group was drunk on new wine.

Peter stood in the middle of the group to explain it was too early for anyone to be drunk but rather they were witnessing an outpouring of the Holy Spirit, as prophesied by the prophet Joel (Acts 2:16-21; Joel 2:18-32). Apparently, the message Peter announced to the multitude was repeated by different disciples in their new language they were now speaking. Everyone could understand what Peter was saying. While not all the specific details of Joel's prophecy were fulfilled on the Day of Pentecost, enough were present to confirm that the crowd was witnessing something similar to the outpouring of the Spirit Joel described. Many Bible teachers believe that the ultimate outpouring will take place at the second coming of Christ.

DEFINITION OF REVIVAL

Revival is God pouring out His presence on His people.

Exponential revival is God pouring out an abundance of power and energy on His people in His church, so it carries the Good News to all available people, through all available methods, at all available times, giving abundant glory to God. The outpouring of the Holy Spirit has been largely ignored by Christians throughout the centuries, except during times of evangelical revival in the church. While the Holy Spirit is a person, the Scriptures sometimes portray Him as being "poured out" like water upon thirsty people in need of My blessing. It's a period of spiritual intensity when the presence of the Holy Spirit is working. The church experiences a work of revival. An outpouring of the Holy Spirit is most often accompanied by an awakening in the unsaved to their need for salvation, and believers recommit themselves to holy living and sacrificial service.

When Peter said, "This is what was spoken by the prophet Joel" (Acts 2:16, *NKJV*), he was describing that the revival in Jerusalem was a prototype of revival that would happen many times in the church age. While many Christians claim they would like to experience revival in their church and community, most are convinced revival will not likely come. But revival is one of the ways I energize a church to effectively reach its community. Revival can come to any church if they are prepared to meet the conditions I have tied to an outpouring of the Holy Spirit. Ironically, many of the reasons people believe their church could never experience revival are really indicators I am ready to do something special in their midst.

THE MESSAGE OF A REVIVED CHURCH

As Peter explained the signs of that day, he pointed to an even greater sign that had taken place a few days earlier. He pointed to My crucifixion: "People of Israel, listen! God publicly endorsed Jesus the Nazarene by doing powerful miracles, wonders, and signs through him, as you well know. But God knew what would happen, and his prearranged plan was carried out when Jesus was betrayed. With the help of lawless Gentiles, you nailed him to a cross and killed him. But God released him from the horrors of death and raised him back to life, for death could not keep him in its grip" (Acts 2:22-24, *NLT*).

Peter explained the meaning of the Old Testament that I had explained to him. He also explained the meaning of the crucifixion and resurrection in the context of two familiar messianic psalms (Ps. 16:8-11; 110:1). Just as Peter and the other disciples had not understood the real significance of these psalms until after I opened their understanding (Luke 24:25), so too many of those who heard Peter preach on Pentecost had never before thought the Messiah would suffer and be raised from the dead. Peter explained these psalms could not logically be applied to David who first penned these words because the corrupted remains of David's body were still in David's tomb. He announced the prophecy applied to Me because I rose from the dead. That made Me unique. He concluded, "Therefore let all the house of Israel know assuredly that God has made this Jesus, whom you crucified, both Lord and Christ" (Acts 2:36).

Many who heard Peter's logical explanation were deeply convicted of their sin. The Greek verb *katenugesan,* which is translated "to cut" (Acts 2:37), was a term used by classical writers to report the devastation of a city by an invading army. Peter's words had brought about a conviction so severe that the people stood devastated in their heart before God the Father. Desperately, they wanted to do something; they cried out, "What shall we do?" (Acts 2:37, *NKJV*)

Peter called them to repent from their sin and trust Me as their Messiah. The outward evidence of such an inner response to the gospel would be submitting to what has become known as Christian baptism: "Let every one of you be baptized in the name of Jesus Christ for the remission of sins; and you shall receive the gift of the Holy Spirit" (Acts 2:38, *NKJV*). Then Peter indicated the outpouring of the Spirit being experienced that day would not be limited to that day or city: "For the promise is to you and to your children and to all who are afar off, as many as the Lord our God will call" (Acts 2:39, *NKJV*).

That day, about three thousand people eagerly responded to Peter's message and were baptized. The infant church in Jerusalem exploded in growth. Because of the Jews' tendency to send only the head of the household to Jerusalem during the feasts, the church was predominantly male in its early days. Many who responded may have been in town only for the feast and within days left Jerusalem to carry the message of My death and resurrection back to their hometowns and cities. Those converted would spread the gospel in other parts of Judea and to the known world.

REACHING OUT TO OTHERS

Those who made decisions to identify with Me and My church were deeply committed: "They continued steadfastly in the apostles' doctrine and fellowship, and in the breaking of bread, and in prayers" (Acts 2:42, *NKJV*). A spirit of community quickly developed to the point that they freely shared their possessions with others in the group. Because of the size of the group, there were few places where they could meet together. They met daily in the temple as a larger group celebrating their newly found faith, but also met in smaller groups in homes throughout the city to nurture the fellowship that had developed within the church. And there were others, who were not converted on Pentecost but were saved later: "and the Lord added to the church daily those who were being saved" (Acts 2:47, *NKJV*).

The evangelistic outreach on the Day of Pentecost was not the only example of mass evangelism. A little later, about 3:00 one afternoon, Peter and John were unexpectedly involved in another large evangelistic outreach. They were on their way to the temple to pray when they were approached by a lame beggar, begging for alms at the gate of the temple. Neither of the disciples had funds to give the beggar, but that did not stop Peter. Once he had the beggar's attention, Peter explained, "Silver and gold I do not have, but what I do have I give you: In the name of Jesus Christ of Nazareth, rise up and walk" (Acts 3:6). Then Peter took the beggar by the hand and lifted him to his feet.

Suddenly the beggar felt strength returning to the bones in his ankles and feet. He not only stood but also jumped and walked around the temple with the two apostles, praising God the Father. In his enthusiasm, his worship attracted a crowd. This beggar was well known at the gate of the temple, and those who gathered around wondered what had happened. He was standing in the temple. Peter soon perceived that some in the crowd were beginning to conclude he had a special power that resulted in this amazing miracle. Eager to set the record straight, Peter stood in Solomon's Porch and used the occasion to once again preach the gospel.

The focus of his message was My crucifixion and resurrection. Peter pulled no punches in clearly affixing the blame for My death on them. After reminding his listeners that Pilate had attempted to release Me, Peter noted, "But you denied the Holy One and the Just, and asked for a murderer to be granted to you, and killed the Prince of life, whom God raised from the dead, of which we are witnesses" (Acts 3:14-15). As in his previous sermon, Peter again called on those who heard him to repent and "be converted, that your sins may be blotted out" (Acts 3:19). Many who heard him believed in Me for salvation. About five thousand men were actively involved with the church at Jerusalem (Acts 4:4).

WHEN THE GOING GOT TOUGH

There was also another response to Peter's preaching: the priests and Sadducees. The Pharisees had been in control of the Sanhedrin when I was crucified, but it was perceived they botched the job, so the Sadducees assumed control. They tended to deny the supernatural in their concept of religion and were "greatly disturbed that they taught the people and preached in Jesus the resurrection from the dead" (Acts 4:2, *NKJV*). Had Peter avoided references to the resurrection in his message, he and John probably would not have been arrested. But the gospel without the resurrection is not the gospel, and the two apostles and the man who had been healed were taken into custody and spent the night in jail.

The next day, the high priests and other leading Jewish leaders met to discuss the matter. They brought the three men out to inquire as to the source of their miraculous power to heal the lame. Peter wasted no time getting to the heart of the gospel: "Let it be known to you all, and to all the people of Israel, that by the name of Jesus Christ of Nazareth, whom you crucified, whom God raised from the dead, by Him this man stands here before you whole" (Acts 4:10, *NKJV*). He went on to stress salvation could only be found in My name, Jesus (v. 12).

Those who heard the apostles speak that day were perplexed. Without a doubt, these men were fishermen and had no formal theological education. It was also obvious "that they had been with Jesus" (Acts 4:13, *NKJV*). When they were dismissed from the room in which the hearing was being conducted, the Sanhedrin began discussing their options. Obviously, a significant miracle had occurred that could not reasonably be denied. They decided their best hope was to convince the apostles not to talk to others about Me. When they pronounced their sentence, the apostles would not agree to it: "Whether it is right in the sight of God to listen to you more than to God, you judge. For we cannot but speak the things which we have seen and heard" (Acts 4:19, 20, *NKJV*). The council threatened them further but eventually released the apostles without punishing them. They realized the miracle had broad popular support and chose not to alienate the people by punishing the ones through whom the miracle was accomplished.

When they were released, Peter and John reported to the church all that had taken place. When the Christians heard, they all prayed for boldness to continue to be faithful in proclaiming the message: "Now, Lord, look on their threats, and grant to Your servants that with all boldness they may speak Your word" (Acts 4:29, *NKJV*).

I answered their request: "And when they had prayed, the place where they were assembled together was shaken; and they were all filled with the Holy Spirit, and they spoke the word of God with boldness" (Acts 4:31, *NKJV*).

In the face of opposition, the quality of their fellowship continued to grow along with their numbers: "Now the multitude of those who believed were of one heart and one soul; neither did anyone say that any of the things he possessed was his own, but they had all things in common" (Acts 4:32, *NKJV*). In one example of corporate sharing, a converted Levite named Joses earned the nickname Barnabas, meaning "Son of Encouragement," and sold his real estate holdings in Cyprus to meet the needs of others.

As the church continued growing, its ministry expanded, touching more lives than before. The ministry reached beyond Jerusalem to the surrounding cities. Yet with the success of the ministry, they were once again attacked by the Sadducees. The apostles were arrested and put in prison. During the evening, they were released by an angel. When the officers arrived the next morning, they found the prison shut up and well guarded, but no prisoners were inside. While the leading priests attempted to understand what was going on, they received a report claiming, "The men whom you put in prison are standing in the temple and teaching the people!" (Acts 5:25, *NKJV*).

The officers were sent to arrest them. When the apostles were brought before the council, they were immediately accused: "Did we not strictly command you not to teach in this name? And look, you have filled Jerusalem with your doctrine, and intend to bring this Man's blood on us!" (Acts 5:28, *NKJV*). But the apostles were not intimidated by the council: "We ought to obey God rather than men" (Acts 5:29, *NKJV*). Then once again they reminded the Sanhedrin of the essence of their message: "The God of our fathers raised up Jesus whom you murdered by hanging on a tree" (Acts 5:30, *NKJV*).

SATURATION EVANGELISM

Although the expression had not yet been coined, the church in Jerusalem practiced what had been previously called saturation evangelism. Today it is called exponential evangelism, which involves preaching the pospel to every available person, at every available time, by every available means or methods. This definition comes from "filling Jerusalem with the gospel." Exponential evangelism is successful because it contacts people where they are, keeps on contacting people, and never stops contacting people. Churches thata practice exponential evangelism make winning people for salvation a passion.

The message of exponential evangelism is the gospel. Paul later summarized the message of the gospel when he wrote, "Christ died for our sins according to the Scriptures, and that He was buried, and that He rose again the third day according to the Scriptures" (1 Cor. 15:3, 4, *NKJV*). When a church practices aggressive evangelism, their message consistently points people to Me.

The target of exponential evangelism is people. An evangelist once expressed frustration after conducting an evangelistic meeting where the host church did everything except ensure unsaved people were present. When a church practices exponential evangelism, people are the focus, not programs. Church programs are designed to reach people. If they are ineffective in accomplishing that purpose, change them to become more effective or replace them with a new and effective way to reach people.

The force of exponential evangelism is found in touching the lost in your community. Evangelism is not limited to a weekly evening visitation team or Saturday morning outreach effort. New Testament evangelism makes sharing the gospel a priority every hour of every day. Churches using this strategy must look to the example of the church at Jerusalem: "Daily in the temple, and in every house, they did not cease teaching and preaching Jesus as the Christ" (Acts 5:42, *NKJV*).

The strategy of saturation evangelism is varied. Whereas many evangelistic churches use one or two effective evangelism strategies, churches that practice exponential evangelism are always looking for new ways to reach people for salvation. They design church ads to reach people and widely distribute gospel literature to tell My story. Keep the name of your church constantly before the public.

Look for ways to use the local media to saturate your town with your message, using radio, television and the print media simultaneously.

SATURATION IS EXPONENTIAL

Evangelism involves communicating the gospel in the power of the Holy Spirit to unconverted people with the intent of effecting conversions. When a church builds its ministry around the Great Commission, those who repent of their sin and trust Me as Savior are encouraged to serve Me as part of the fellowship of that local church. New believers become part of the team to reach others for salvation.

The story of My exponential church at Jerusalem reveals there are no practical limits to church size and there are no limits to evangelism. By the end of the Day of Pentecost, there were 3,000 involved in the church. In the later days, "the Lord added to the church daily" (Acts 2:47, *NKJV*). Very soon that number grew to 5,000 men (not counting women and children). Before long, "the number of the disciples was multiplying" (Acts 6:1, *NKJV*). Notice the change in the arithmetic terms from adding to multiplying. According to the historical records of the time, it is estimated that eventually about half of the 200,000 people then living in Jerusalem were converted to Me and added to that church.

The light that shines farthest shines brightest at home. I told My disciples, "The field is the world" (Matt. 13:38, *NKJV*). Even if a church managed to reach 100 percent of the people living in their community, they have still not saturated the world with the gospel. I also said, "Let us go into the next towns, that I may preach there also, because for this purpose I have come forth" (Mark 1:38, *NKJV*).

Even as the church in Jerusalem grew, it reached out beyond its city limits: "Also a multitude gathered from the surrounding cities to Jerusalem, bringing sick people and those who were tormented by unclean spirits, and they were healed" (Acts 5:16, *NKJV*). The church at Jerusalem established new churches in area cities even before the persecution intensified. It is clear that the practice of evangelizing area towns intensified when the persecution forced many to flee to other cities to escape the persecution (Acts 8:1, 4).

Chapter Three

I AM JESUS:
A Witnessing Church

"But you will receive power when the Holy Spirit comes upon you. And you will be my witnesses, telling people about me everywhere—in Jerusalem, throughout Judea, in Samaria, and to the ends of the earth."

ACTS 1:8, *NLT*

I gave the Great Commission to My eleven disciples and the church grew. Each went out to communicate his/her faith to another person, so they prayed, witnessed, and shared the gospel, winning people into the family of God. Then, each person they won was responsible to win someone else. Their strategy resulted in planting churches with the confidence that every growing thing reproduces itself. So each church they planted would begin another church.

The church at Jerusalem and all the churches planted from Jerusalem grew because of exponential evangelism—which means two areas of evangelism: first, exponential personal evangelism. Notice in this chapter where new believers were won to Me by those previously won to Me on the day of Pentecost. But second, it was exponential church planting evangelism. Every new church then went out to plant another church. That's exponential growth.

For 40 days of post-resurrection ministry, I taught My disciples the truths of the gospel and the new distinctives of the church. Then came the 40th day, the last day I would spend physically with My disciples. They forgot all about what I taught; they had questions about the Old Testament.

"Lord, will you at this time restore the kingdom to Israel?" (Acts 1:6, *NKJV*). When I wanted them to look forward to the church, they wanted to look back at the kingdom.

"It is not for you to know times or seasons which the Father has put in His own authority," I responded (Acts 1:7, *NKJV*). I knew their intentions were good, but there was a greater priority for them. I would return, but while I was away, they had work to do.

"You shall be witnesses to Me" (Acts 1:8, *NKJV*). That was their commission in a nutshell. As they waited for the future kingdom, they were to be My witnesses. The task would be to tell others what they had seen and heard and experienced. I had already told them the Holy Spirit would work in the lives of unsaved people around them (John 16:7-11). Soon, the Holy Spirit would come upon them in a unique way.

Sometimes, the last thing a person says before he leaves is the most important thing to remember. As the disciples stood on the Mount of Olives that day, they must have realized they were experiencing a life-transforming moment. The things I was saying were really important. From this point on, they would use one word to define who they were. They were "witnesses."

The word "witness" is one of several terms in Scripture to describe the process called *evangelism*. Evangelism is communicating the gospel in an understandable manner and motivating the person to believe in Me and become a responsible member of My church. Evangelism is perhaps the most exciting experience in which you will ever be involved. There is a sense of personal fulfilment and inner joy when you effectively share your faith with others. The Father wants all involved in evangelism.

Various people picture different things when they think of an evangelist. For some, an evangelist is a famous preacher who travels from city to city preaching the gospel. Others think of the host or hostess of a popular religious television program. Still others think of those brave church members who go door to door to talk to strangers about the gospel. Too often you define effective evangelism according to your stereotyped pictures of an evangelistic ministry. But the real key to effective evangelism is not found in a *program* but rather a *person*. You the individual share your faith with another. You don't talk about Christian laws, i.e., the *Four Spiritual Laws*; but you talk about Me, "I am the way ... the truth ... and the life" (John 14:6, *KJV*), of salvation. Salvation is a personal experience. You accept Me—a Person—as your personal Savior.

Evangelism is best captured in My use of the word *witness*. An effective witness has seen, heard and experienced something, then they share with others what they experienced. Their witness comes out of the overflow of their life. In that context, every Christian is a witness.

The Christians of the early church chose to ignore excuses about witnessing. The result of their faithful witness, and that of Christians in every generation since, is that others hear the gospel. It is now entrusted to you to pass it on to your generation and those who follow you.

To make sure the world is evangelized, I made all believers witnesses, so no generation would ever be ignorant of "the wonderful works of God" (Acts 2:11, *NKJV*). With such an important responsibility in your hands, you should do all you can to be a credible witness to those you meet.

DEVELOPING A CREDIBLE WITNESS

Those who are most effective in their witness of the Christian faith are those who have developed a lifestyle that lends credibility to what they say. When they share their faith with others, it seems like the most natural thing for them to do. And those who hear them seem to be wanting to know more about how they too can experience a personal relationship with God the Father.

What makes these people who witness for Me so unique? Are they born this way, or can anyone learn to witness? If witnessing can be learned, is it possible to become a more effective witness? The Bible has much to say about the kind of person who is effective in evangelism. The good news is that it is possible for all Christians to develop a credible witness.

The most effective witness is one that flows out of a maturing Christian life. As you grow into a deeper relationship with God the Father by dealing with problems in your life, you will be more effective in sharing your faith with others (Ps. 51:10-13). People are going to be more responsive to the gospel if they see Me working in your life than if you merely share abstract principles with others.

Part of the maturing process involves developing a genuine spiritual concern for others. This is called a burden that keeps you faithfully sharing your faith with others (Ps. 126:6). Certainly, one of the keys to Paul's success in evangelism was his concern for those who did not know Me as Savior (Rom. 9:1-3; 10:1).

Many Christians are effective in sharing their faith because they clearly understand My love (2 Cor. 5:14). People do things for love they would not do for any other reason, and they do it with more passion than they might otherwise. You begin when you realize just how much I love you, then you naturally share My love with others (1 John 4:9, 19; Rom 5:5).

Perhaps when you appreciate My love, you develop a servant's heart toward others. Your willingness to help people adds to your credibility as you share the gospel (1 Cor. 9:22).

The effective witness believes in the power of the gospel to make a positive difference in others' lives (Rom. 1:16). When people come to faith in Me, they become a new creation (2 Cor. 5:17). The one who has personally experienced this change in his or her own life is more likely to recognize the life-changing potential of the gospel in the lives of others (1 Tim. 1:12-15).

People listen to a witness when they seek a positive difference I make in their lifestyle. This is especially true when they see the different way you respond to problems because everyone struggles with trouble in this life. Peter reminded Christians to be prepared in the midst of their suffering to explain My gospel to those who ask (1 Pet. 3:14-17). He realized people would be attracted to Me when they saw the positive way Christians respond to problems. When unsaved family members see your consistent Christian witness, they are often won to salvation even without someone explaining the gospel (1 Pet. 3:1).

Those most effective in evangelism tend to exercise wisdom in approaching people to discuss salvation (Dan. 12:3). They have acquired spiritual insight that makes them more effective in dealing with people (Prov. 11:30). This insight is also available to all believers. When you recognize a need for greater wisdom in your own life, you can get it by asking the Father (Jas. 1:5). Also, when you make personal Bible study an ongoing spiritual discipline in your life, you establish another means by which I provide you with My wisdom (Ps. 19:7).

WITNESSING WITH POWER

Because effective evangelism is done in the power of the Holy Spirit, you acquire unique spiritual power through the fullness of the Holy Spirit, i.e., "Be filled with the Spirit" (Eph. 5:18, *NKJV*). In the New Testament, a believer's spiritual power in witnessing was evidence of the fullness of the Holy Spirit (Acts 1:8). You can obtain spiritual power by (1) wanting to be filled with the Holy Spirit, (2) repenting of known sin in your life, (3) asking for the filling of the Holy Spirit, and (4) trusting Me to fill you and use you (John 7:37-39).

The same Holy Spirit who empowers you to be effective in witnessing also empowered the Scriptures to be effective in saving people (2 Tim. 3:15). One of the expressions used to describe the Scriptures is "word of life" (Phil. 2:16, *NKJV*) because the Bible is the Word of God that produces spiritual life in others. Many effective witnesses commit *Scripture to memory* to use when sharing the plan of salvation (Ps. 19:7). It is always easier to get a job done right when you have the right tools. In the work of witnessing, the Scriptures are its tools.

There is something addictive about sharing the gospel with others. As you begin sharing your faith with others, something happens to you internally. Wanting to tell others about Me can become a natural response because you get an inner sense of fulfilment and joy. Before long, you find yourself enjoying witnessing so much that you can barely conceive of not being involved in it (1 Cor. 9:16). What may seem so intimidating today can become a passionate part of your Christian life and ministry.

THE WAY OF SALVATION

Salvation is as simple as a relationship with Me; you put your faith in Me. The Bible says, "Look . . . and be . . . saved" (Isa. 45:22, *NKJV*). Look and live. When you look to Me to answer your sin problem, you live for eternity. Yet the theologians have made salvation complicated.

Not every church member will go to heaven; yet most have declared they believe in God or they believe in Me: "Many will say to Me in the day, 'Lord, Lord,' have we not . . . in Thy name, and done many wonders in Your name? And then will I profess unto them, 'I never knew you; depart from Me, you who practice lawlessness'" (Matt. 7:22-23, *NKJV*). Obviously, some who think they are going to heaven will not make it. They know "religious" answers, but that is not enough.

Salvation is pictured as a road; you take steps along this road to get to heaven: "Enter ye in at the strait gate: for wide is the gate, and broad is the way, that leadeth to destruction, and many there be which go in there at: Because strait is the gate, and narrow is the way, which leadeth unto life, and few there be that find it" (Matt. 7:13-14, *KJV*). Remember I said, "I am the way, the truth, and the life. No one comes to the Father except through Me" (John 14:6, *NKJV*).

Early Christianity in the book of Acts referred to as the "way" (9:2). I am the "way" to God the Father. In approaching Him you must take four steps; no more and no less.

1. *Know your need.* People do not turn to God the Father until they feel a need for Him. And this compulsion is not felt until they realize that their paths will lead to destruction: "For all have sinned, and fall short of the glory of God" (Rom. 3:23, *NKJV*). The word "all" includes every human of all ages, it includes you.

A minister once tried to convince a small boy he was a sinner, but the boy would not admit it.

"Have you ever lied to your Mommy?" the preacher asked. The boy shook his head no.

"Have you ever taken anything that didn't belong to you or fought with your brother or sister?" Again the boy shook his head no.

"He's sinning to you now," observed his older brother.

He knew his little brother was guilty of these actions. The Bible says we ALL have sinned. You will never turn to the Father until you first realize you are a sinner.

2. *Know your punishment.* In your society many don't worry about those who break a law until they hurt someone else, but My laws are different: "For the wages of sin is death, but the gift of God is eternal life in Christ Jesus our Lord" (Rom. 6:23, *NKJV*). The Father punishes every offense. Because you have sinned, you will pay the penalty.

When you break a speed law, you don't get caught for every offense, but if you speed through a radar trap, you pay the fine. Along this line of thought, you never escape the Father's radar for He catches every offense; and the penalty is death.

"Even for one sin?" a woman asked at a church altar. The pastor showed her, "For whosoever shall keep the whole law, and yet offend in one point, he is guilty of all" (Jas. 2:10, *NKJV*). One sin makes you a sinner.

You get wages for your work; *wages* are what you have coming to you: "The wages of sin is death" (Rom. 6:23a, *NKJV*). This verse shows you have death or hell coming because you have sinned. In contrast, "the gift of God is eternal life" (6:23b, *NKJV*). The gift is free and undeserved; it is not wages. You get death for your sins, yet God the Father gives you life as a *gift*.

3. *Know the gospel*: "But God demonstrates His own love toward us, in that while we were still sinners, Christ died for us" (Rom. 5:8, *NKJV*). God the Father has given Me to die for your sins. This is the gospel. *Gospel* means "good news," and the greatest news ever is that I save.

The gospel has two aspects: propositional truth and personal truth. First, propositional truth reflects the truth on paper—it is written in your doctrinal statements. This gospel is My plan for salvation. Paul defined it: "I declare to you the gospel which I preached to you, which also you received and in which you stand, by which also you are saved . . . that Christ died for our sins according to the Scriptures, and that He was buried, and that He rose again the third day according to the Scriptures" (1 Cor. 15:1-4). The gospel explains My death, burial, and resurrection. I died for you.

4. *Respond to the gospel*. The gospel is more than propositional truth; it is personal truth. This is truth existing in a person. I am that person. I am Jesus Christ. When you accept this truth, you do more than give mental assent to My death, burial, and resurrection. You accept Me as your Savior. The gospel becomes personal when

you invite Me into your life: "But as many as received him, to them gave he power to become the sons of God" (John 1:12, *KJV*).

Some have a correct doctrinal statement, but if they have not received Me, Jesus Christ, they are not saved. Others claim to know Me as a person; yet, when their experience is not backed up with correct doctrine, they are misled. Belief in Me is finding My way to heaven. When you find it, you must do something about it: "That if you confess with your mouth the Lord Jesus and believe in your heart that God has raised Him from the dead, you will be saved" (Rom. 10:9, *NKJV*). You respond by belief in the heart and a confession of the mouth.

SALVATION—A TOTAL EXPERIENCE

Belief is not only head knowledge. It involves your total response to Me. When you get on a jetliner, you can't place only one leg on the plane and fly to another city. You must respond completely by placing yourself wholly in the plane. Salvation is the same total experience. You must put your complete trust in Me, Jesus Christ, trusting Me to take you to heaven. This involves your intellect, emotion, and will.

1. *Using the intellect is the first step of experience.* A person must know God the Father's plan of salvation before he/she can accept it. Just as you cannot communicate to another person apart from understanding, the Father follows the same law: He cannot communicate with you unless you understand Our plan of salvation.

Knowledge involves awareness and understanding, but knowledge does not convert your soul. I illustrated this point: "Not everyone that saith unto me, 'Lord, Lord,' shall enter into the kingdom of heaven; but he that doeth the will of my Father which is in heaven" (Matt. 7:21, *NKJV*). Those people had knowledge but it did little good: "I never knew you" (Matt. 7:23, *NKJV*), even though they had head knowledge.

2. *The stirring of emotions is the second step of experience.* People are emotional beings. They feel deeply about many issues. You cannot neglect the part emotion plays in your conversion, although not everyone will express emotions openly. Some clap their hands and sing for joy. Others weep and agonize. On the other hand, some are converted without any outward display of emotions.

A man in Roanoke, Virginia, confessed to his wife that he had committed adultery. In a blinding rage, she ripped the curtains from the window, broke all the dishes, and announced she was suing for divorce. The next Sunday morning the couple attended church and, during the invitation, he went forward, crying like a brokenhearted lover. A few minutes later she followed him to the altar. After the service was over, those who stood around were embarrassed by their hugs and kisses. Theirs was an emotional salvation—emotional both before and after receiving Me as Savior.

A Certified Public Accountant analyzed the gospel and received salvation. Later a pastor confessed, "I didn't think he was saved because he didn't show any feelings." Yet the man became one of the greatest workers in his church.

What place do emotions have in conversion? You should never judge a man's seriousness by his tears at the altar. Felix trembled and answered, "Go thy way for this time; when I have a convenient season, I will call for thee" (Acts 24:25, *KJV*).

His emotions were stirred, just as some who weep yet never are saved. You cannot judge the sincerity of a person by the outward display of emotions. The country preacher said it eloquently: "The toot of the car's horn doesn't tell you how much gas is in the tank."

Just because a person does not cry or show joy doesn't mean he lacks sincerity. Many people keep their emotions to themselves, yet they feel deeply.

Just as knowledge alone cannot save, so too religious emotionalism will not get a man to heaven. Emotions are used to motivate a person to seek relief. Some are terrified of judgment and seek salvation. Others are overwhelmed with love. Other emotions that might make a person seek salvation are guilt, gratitude, pressure, or uncertainty.

Emotions, like repentance, are an outward manifestation of My inner work of salvation. After a person is saved, he might experience feelings of relief, joy, or tears of happiness.

3. *The response of the will is the third step of experience.* There is nothing a person can do to save himself—I, Jesus Christ, have done it all. But a person must respond with their inner being to accept salvation.

Faith is believing in Me. You know what I did on the cross and you accept it. Your feelings are stirred by the convicting work of the Holy Spirit and you respond by an act of the will. You express biblical faith.

When a person will respond in belief, it is an act of obedience to Me: "But ye have obeyed from the heart that form of doctrine which was delivered you" (Rom. 6:17, *KJV*). The will must say yes.

Repentance is necessary for salvation, but repentance does not save you. Like the bus ticket that reads "This half good for passage, not good if detached," salvation is good for passage to heaven, but salvation is not salvation if detached from repentance. The second half of the bus ticket reads, "Not good for passage; keep in your possession until arriving at destination." This ticket stub represents repentance: not good for passage to heaven; keep doing good works until you get to your destination.

Eternal life does not begin with repentance for these are dead works that cannot merit you before God the Father. Your eternal life begins when I come into your heart. When you hear the preaching of the gospel, it is God's Word that stirs the heart.

Conviction stirs the spirit to respond to God the Father, "For the word of God is quick, and powerful . . . and is a discerner of the thoughts and intents of the heart" (Heb. 4:12, *KJV*). The Word of

God lays bare your sin that is hidden in your thoughts. Your sin is never hidden from God the Father, but the Bible convicts you by illuminating the mind, showing your sinfulness.

Conviction begins deep in the mind and moves to your consciousness. A person becomes aware that they have offended God the Father. The effect is that they cry, tremble, or become reflective. Sad stories or persuasive arguments will not bring conviction. It comes from the Word of God by the Holy Spirit. The Holy Spirit convicted you of sin (John 16:8) because you had not believed in Me (John 16:9). He also performed the same work of conviction in your heart concerning righteousness and judgment (John 16:8-10).

Tears will not convince God the Father of your sincerity, nor will your smile convince others that you have an inner peace. The stirring of the emotions is a necessary concomitant of salvation, not salvation itself. You must respond.

Your mind knows the facts of the gospel and your emotions motivate you, but your will must respond. Paul describes this: "Ye have obeyed from the heart that form of doctrine" (Rom. 6:17, *KJV*). Other descriptive verbs are used to show this response: receiving Me, accepting the Lord, asking Me into your heart, placing your trust in Me, or taking Me by faith. Each of these statements means you have made a volitional act of your will in turning your life over to Me.

A young man was dealing for the first time with a seeker at the church altar. He told the person to pray, "Dear Jesus, come into my heart." When they got up, the soul-winner thought of an extra prayer. They returned to the altar where he instructed the seeker to pray, "Dear Jesus, forgive me of my sins."

As they returned to the first pew, he thought of a third prayer: "Dear Jesus, take me to heaven." Actually, people are saved by using any one of the three formulas. I am not as interested in the words of your mouth as I am in the attitude of your heart.

So, to be truly saved, you must *know the content* of the *gospel, respond by your emotions,* and make a *decision of your will* to turn your life over to Me.

Chapter Four

I AM JESUS:
A Teaching Church

"Therefore, go and make disciples of all the nations, baptizing them in the name of the Father and the Son and the Holy Spirit. Teach these new disciples to obey all the commands I have given you. And be sure of this: I am with you always, even to the end of the age."

MATTHEW 28:19-20, *NLT*

Paul was forced by the continued opposition from the Jews to leave Thessalonica to travel west to the city of Berea. Here, Paul found people open to his preaching, willing to give careful consideration to the Word of God. The Bereans were "more fair-minded than those in Thessalonica, in that they received the word with all readiness of mind, and searched the Scriptures daily to find out whether these things were so" (Acts 17:11, *NKJV*).

Paul's preaching of the gospel to a group that was open to study of the Scriptures reflects the exponential church. Because of his Bible-teaching ministry, "many of them believed, and also not a few of the Greeks, prominent women as well as men" (v. 12, *NKJV*). Those converted in Berea came to faith in Christ through the careful study of the Scriptures. As a result, more here than in other places, the Berean Christians had a strong faith grounded in the Word of God.

Paul's adversaries from Thessalonica "learned that the Word of God was preached by Paul at Berea, they came there also and stirred up the crowds" (Acts 17:13, *NKJV*). Paul realized the opposition was directed primarily at him and that his continued presence in that community would sooner or later make the Berean Christians themselves targets of persecution. Paul faced a difficult choice. If he stayed in Berea, he could teach them to continue growing as Christians, but he might also make them targets of the persecution he was experiencing. If he left, the Christians might be safe, but would the foundation he laid remain firm?

Paul's ministry in Berea was consistent with the Great Commission where I commanded, "Teaching them to observe all things I have commanded you" (Matt. 28:20, *NKJV*). The Bereans were able to develop a strong church because it was planted in a teaching environment.

THE CITY OF BEREA

The Roman senator Cicero once described the city of Berea as being "out of the way," a town in the district of Emathia, in southwestern Macedonia. It was located at the foot of Mount Bermius on the tributary of the Haliacmon River. Looking toward the southern horizon, they could see the snow-capped peak of Mount Olympus. Berea was far enough inland that life tended to move at a slower pace than in the busier coastal city.

While emperor worship was the law of the land, it was a law that tended to be enforced more often in seats of Roman authority and less elsewhere like in Berea. The Jews were free to worship God in the synagogue with limited interference.

When Paul arrived, Paul followed his usual custom of preaching in the synagogue. His sermon had deep roots in the Old

Testament. In Berea he found a group eager to study the Scriptures; he was even more eager to teach. It is not surprising that people not only came to faith in Christ in Berea but also experienced significant spiritual growth.

LEARNING FROM THE BEREANS

The Berean Christians' model suggests five steps for personal and church Bible study.

"These (Bereans) were more fair-minded than those in Thessalonica, in that they received the word with all readiness, and searched the Scriptures daily to find out whether these things were so" (Acts 17:11, *NKJV*).

The first description of the Berean Christians suggests they were *yielded to Me* in their approach to the Scriptures. They "received the Word." As you approach Bible study, you also need to do so the same. Be willing to receive and apply any and all biblical principles found in the Scriptures to your life.

Second, the Bereans were *intentional in Bible study*. They came to the Scriptures "with all readiness," looking for truth. They had an eager mind, also described as a hungry spirit. It was not a matter of reading a chapter to fulfill their Christian duty but rather a desire or pursuit of Scripture for a better understanding of Me.

Third, the Bereans approached Bible study with a *word-by-word study* of the Scriptures. They "searched" the Scriptures in their pursuit of truth. Theirs was not a superficial reading, but digging into the meaning of words. The word *searched* means "sift" as a baker sifting flour to separate each particle from every other particle. When you study the Bible word for word, you are sifting every particle of Scripture to make you understand what I am saying. As you invest time looking up the meaning of words and expressions used in Scripture, you gain insights missed by those who gloss over details in their study of the Scriptures.

The fourth characteristic of the Bereans was their routine of *daily Bible study*. Each day these Christians had a fresh encounter with Me through their study of the Scriptures. On a daily basis they were reminded of the heavenly Father's merciful compassion toward His people (Lam. 3:22, 23). Just as I instructed My disciples to pray for daily bread (Matt. 6:11), so to you need to go daily to the Scriptures, which are the Bread of Life.

The fifth characteristic of the Bereans was their *purpose in Bible study*. There was something the Bereans wanted to know as they came to the Scriptures. They studied "to find out whether these things were so." This verse tells you to analyze Bible content. This will lead to assurance. They wanted confidence from their Bible study. Likewise, you would be wise to follow their example in your own Bible study.

When you study the Bible, look for the content of a message from the heavenly Father. You want a message that can be trusted. With that attitude, you get confidence in what you hear from Him. Ask the Father to open your eyes to give you insight into what you read. The psalmist prayed, "Open my eyes, that I may see wondrous things from Your law" (Ps. 119:18, *NKJV*). If sin is hindering your relationship with Me, it should be confessed so that you might be cleansed (1 John 1:9). Then as you read, you need to listen carefully to what I am saying to you (1 Sam. 3:10). Even as you begin, you need to be prepared to obey what I am telling you through your personal Bible study (Acts 9:6).

KNOWING ME THROUGH SCRIPTURE

You will take on My characteristics as you study the Bible. Paul tells you, "We all, with unveiled face, beholding as in a mirror the glory of the Lord, are being transformed into the same image from glory to glory" (2 Cor. 3:18, *NKJV*). This verse illustrates you standing before a mirror, which is God's Word. In the mirror you do not see your image, but you see a reflection of Me. The more you study the mirror (Me in the Bible), the more you become like Me.

Take your faith seriously. Set aside a time each day to read, study, meditate and memorize My Word. These four words are stepping stones to master the Bible, "by which have been given to us exceedingly great and precious promises, that through these you may be partakers of the divine nature" (2 Pet. 1:4, *NKJV*). The Bible gives you a new desire.

1. *Read the Bible daily.* Don't leave Bible reading up to your inclination or don't wait until you are ready to study the Bible. Some days you won't feel like reading the Scriptures. You must discipline yourself if you are to grow in Bible knowledge. General Douglas MacArthur claimed, "Believe me, sir, never a night goes by, be I ever so tired, but I read the Word of God before I go to bed." Develop a daily Bible reading plan. You can read the entire Bible in one year if you read four chapters a day.

2. *Bible study is more than reading scripture.* A young Christian is like those in the first grade. They don't know the material or how to study. An effective plan is to begin with a basic Bible reading; it will give you breadth, and study will give you depth.

Begin your study by reading a passage several times. Read the portion in several versions. As you go over the passage, ask these questions in your study, "What is it saying?" Don't read your thoughts into the verse. Ask what the author meant. Interpret each verse in its context.

Next question in your study is: "Where else does God say this?" Use the center column reference in your Bible to find other places teaching the same truth. You may have to use a concordance to find a parallel passage. But comparing scripture with scripture will expand your knowledge of the Bible.

Next in your study ask, "What are the problems in the passage?" You don't want to center your life on problems, but don't overlook any. You solve them by a clear understanding of the problem. Write it out. List what you think the answers might be. Then look in a Bible commentary. The author's explanation may give you an insight in finding the answer.

The final question for Bible study is, "What does it mean to me?" Here you apply the scripture to your life. Think of the ways you could apply these verses to your life. Then write out the principles so you have a clear understanding of the practical application.

You will grow as you analyze words. Look up their meaning in a dictionary. Then look up the word in a concordance to see the way it is used in other references. In-depth word study is an excellent means to grasp biblical doctrine.

When you come to unclear circumstances, look up the geography or social background in an encyclopedia. Don't let anything escape your grasp. When doctrinal problems face you, search for the correct interpretation in a book on doctrine.

3. *The third step in Bible study is memorization.* The psalmist declared, "Your word I have hidden in my heart, that I might not sin against You" (Ps. 119:11, *NKJV*). You will want to memorize portions of Scripture for various reasons. When I was tempted in the wilderness, I quoted Scripture. If you have the Bible in your heart, you can quote the Scripture in your hour of trial. When Philip, a deacon, wanted to witness to the Ethiopian in the chariot, he knew Isaiah 53 and used it to lead the eunuch to salvation. Also, when you must make difficult decisions, My Word will guide you into My will.

Memorize scripture by first marking the verse in your Bible. Underline or highlight the verse so it will stand out the next time you study the passage. Next, write or type the verse on a small card. Carry the card or cards with you for review in free time. Plan a systematic way to review the verses you have already memorized. Without review you cannot remember the exact words that you memorized. You may even forget the whole verse. But you will grow in the process of applying diligent effort to master the verse and its meaning.

4. *Meditation is thinking about the truth of the verse,* or go over and over the words in your mind. The psalmist indicated that the growing Christian is like the growing tree, prospering because of meditation: "Blessed is the man Who walks not in the counsel of the ungodly, nor stands in the path of sinners, Nor sits in the seat of the scornful; but his delight is in the law of the Lord, and in His law he meditates day and night" (Ps. 1:1-2, *NKJV*). The psalmist continues, "He shall be like a tree planted by the rivers of water, that brings forth its fruit in its season" (Ps. 1:3, *NKJV*).

You should meditate on the Bible because it is a message from Me. A college sophomore got a daily letter from his girlfriend. When he quickly opened it and read it in front of the mailbox, the other guys teased him. He got in the habit of going to his room so he could give full attention to every word she said. That is the way to meditate on the Bible.

Because each word has a significance, and none are there by error, you should meditate on every word. You can spend a lifetime studying the Bible and never exhaust its depth.

SUMMARY AND CONCLUSION

The early church grew because of exponential Bible teaching. What is that? Remember, exponential means rapid growth according to a predetermined formula. Exponential teaching is using every available teaching method to teach every Christian in the church (from children to senior adult, and new believers to mature believers) at every available time.

The first church is Jerusalem and is an example of this principle. Its exponential growth demonstrated that all believers were grounded in the Word of God and in obedience to Me. The church in Berea illustrates how early churches grew exponentially. Not only did the churches at Jerusalem and Berea and Antioch grow exponentially, but also they did it because they taught the Word of God exponentially.

Chapter Five

I AM JESUS:

A Ministering and Serving Church

"For even the Son of Man came not to be served but to serve others and to give his life as a ransom for many."

MARK 10:45, *NLT*

The new church in Jerusalem was growing. But growth produced problems. The large growing numbers of converts made it difficult to keep up with details of ministry. The apostles couldn't adequately supervise everything. They knew they had to give priority to prayer and the preaching of the gospel. It is not surprising that before long, an internal dissension began to develop.

While the church at Jerusalem was predominantly Jewish in character, it had two different ethnic groups: Palestinian Jews and Hellenistic Jews (those from outside the Holy Land). The Palestinian Jews tended to adhere to the Old Testament law on things like food and social customs, whereas the Hellenistic Jews were more liberal, adopting aspects of Gentile culture into their lifestyle. The normal ethnic tensions between these two groups soon erupted in the new church. The Jews from outside the Holy Land began complaining that their widows were being overlooked as food and other supplies were being distributed.

The offended Jews had a valid point, but the apostles did not have time to personally distribute relief without abandoning their primary task of prayer and preaching. When the murmuring came to the attention of the apostles, they recognized the severe impact this minor problem could have if it was not solved. Therefore, the apostles concluded, "It is not desirable that we should leave the word of God and serve tables" (Acts 6:2, *NKJV*). The apostles proposed that the church select seven men who could be appointed to supervise the distribution to the widows. While the term "deacon" is not used to describe these men in this context, many Bible teachers look at these seven men as the first deacons of the church. In this context, the apostles stressed four essential qualities of these first church officers: (1) a good reputation, (2) full of the Holy Spirit, (3) full of wisdom, (4) full of faith (Acts 6:3, 5).

The church agreed with the apostles and selected seven men. It is interesting to note that each of these men have Greek names and therefore probably had a Hellenistic background. One of the seven is specifically identified as "a proselyte from Antioch" (Acts 6:5). This would make Nicolas the first Gentile church officer. This meant the new church bent over backward to be fair.

Prayers were then offered to put these new servants into ministry. As a result, a problem that threatened the church resulted in strengthening the church: "Then the word of God spread, and the number of disciples multiplied greatly in Jerusalem, and a great many of the priests were obedient to the faith" (Acts 6:7, *NKJV*). The priests who opposed the Christian message because of its focus on My resurrection, embraced the gospel when they realized how the Christian message had changed lives and resolved problems, especially money problems.

CAN I USE LAY PEOPLE IN MINISTRY?

As the newly converted priests became part of the life of the early church, they must have found the church's emphasis on lay ministry somewhat strange. All priests were physical descendants of Aaron, Israel's first High Priest. From the moment they were born, they were prepared for a career involved in some aspect of temple worship. As a son learned his trade from his father, so the son of a priest learned how to be a priest by observing his father. Like other small boys in the community, he attended the local synagogue school. When he got older, he attended one of several recognized schools that trained him in various skills priests were expected to have. At age thirty, he began his active service as a priest.

Christianity differed from Judaism in its view of ministry. I, Jesus, was from the tribe of Judah and therefore would have been considered unqualified to be a priest. I was accepted to teach the law as a rabbi, but My birth disqualified Me as a priest. The priest would have considered Me a lay teacher. When I called disciples, they likewise became lay teachers. Most had developed a business interest long before they followed Me. They too were viewed suspiciously by the religious establishment because they preached without first being trained in a recognized rabbinical school (Acts 4:13).

A POWERFUL STATEMENT

The appointment of seven laymen from the congregation to assist in ministry was a statement that laypeople would be part of ministry in the new church. Most of the 120 in the Upper Room were laymen who had been involved in ministry on the Day of Pentecost. Also, another reason I was adding to the church daily was that all believers were daily witnessing to their friends. When the apostles gathered the congregation to choose seven men, they were employing an innovative practice of using laypeople in ministry. This became the new official policy of the church.

Despite the commitment of the apostles to lay ministry, this approach has not always been followed throughout history.

As various denominations developed schools to train ministers, those ministers often served alongside laypeople in their churches. Before long, manylaypeople realized they were not as well trained as their pastors. Because their pastor did not train them to be more effective in ministry, many laypeople withdrew from ministry and left it to the professionals. As more and more lay people dropped out, the view that laypeople are not needed in ministry became more widely believed.

Throughout history, churches that have developed a clergy approach to ministry have usually become ingrown and ultimately are not able to significantly impact society. In contrast, churches that have emphasized the importance of lay involvement have had a profound impact on their culture. Some of America's largest church denominations are the result of widespread lay ministry within their churches.

Originally in the Old Testament, God the Father wanted everyone in ministry. He wanted Israel to become "a kingdom of priests and a holy nation" (Ex. 19:6, *NKJV*). In the New Testament, Peter uses that same language to describe the church (1 Pet. 2:9). The following examples of two laymen of the seven demonstrate how laypeople can become involved in ministry today.

THE MINISTRY OF STEPHEN

Stephen is the first of the seven described in detail. Even though he was involved with new responsibilities in caring for the widows, he also had other ministry opportunities. Stephen was an able communicator and often disputed in Hellenistic synagogues in Jerusalem, including the Synagogue of the Freedmen. Rabbis and rabbinical students from Asia who came to Jerusalem to study the law attended that synagogue. Many Bible teachers believe that may have also been the synagogue where Saul of Tarsus attended when he was in Jerusalem.

It was not unusual in the synagogues to allow a visitor to teach and then debate their message if it was contrary to what they believed. As a result, the synagogue was a place of lively discussion. Leading teachers in the synagogue would typically challenge what was viewed as doctrinal error, showing the superiority of their own view. But when Stephen preached the gospel in this synagogue, "they were not able to resist the wisdom and the Spirit by which he spoke" (Acts 6:10, *NKJV*).

Because they could not defeat Stephen through the normally effective means of debate in the synagogue, several of the more prominent members of that synagogue secretly arranged to have men report that Stephen was guilty of blasphemy. This was a serious charge and was effective in inciting the people and Jewish leaders against Stephen. He was seized and brought before the council. There, false witnesses accused, "This man does not cease to speak blasphemous words against this holy place and the law; for we have heard him say that this Jesus of Nazareth will destroy this place and change the customs which Moses delivered to us" (Acts 6:13, 14, *NKJV*).

After the witnesses were heard, the whole council focused their attention on Stephen as he presented his defence. Stephen began by reviewing the history of Israel. Like the apostles before him, he charged the council with having rejected Me. His words brought deep conviction to the hearts of the Sanhedrin just as Peter's words on Pentecost had brought similar conviction. But rather than looking for a way to get right with God the Father, the council turned on Stephen with anger. As he continued to speak, "They cried out with a loud voice, stopped their ears, and ran at him with one accord; and they cast him out of the city and stoned him" (Acts 7:57, 58, *NKJV*).

One of those present that day was a young, promising Pharisee named Saul of Tarsus. Later, he claimed that when the balloting was taken to sentence Stephen, "I cast my vote against them" (Acts

26:10, *NKJV*). As others actually stoned Stephen, Saul watched over their coats. Although not on the front line, he must have heard the dying Stephen pray his final words to Me: "Lord, do not charge them with this sin" (Acts 7:60, *NKJV*).

In his career as a Pharisee and member of the Sanhedrin, Saul had probably witnessed several executions, but he had not seen many men die like Stephen. He was probably more accustomed to hearing hardened criminals curse God and the Romans. Many Bible teachers believe Stephen's preaching and death planted a seed that would later produce fruit on the Damascus Road in the conversion of Paul.

Just as Stephen found a place to minister in his community, you can find a place to minister within your community. In most churches, there are always more things to be done than there are people to do them. Often, churches attempt to compensate by having its best workers take on several jobs. While that might help on a temporary basis, long term it produces burned-out workers and perhaps a greater shortage.

THE MINISTRY OF PHILIP

Following the death of Stephen, the persecution of My church intensified. Because the Sanhedrin was based in Jerusalem, the persecution in the city was more intense than in the outlying communities. As people began to recognize this, many believers moved to other communities throughout Judea. Some moved beyond Judea into other regions far from Jerusalem. As they left, they took their Christian faith to new communities that had not yet heard the gospel.

> *"As for Saul, he made havoc of the church, entering every*
> *house, and dragging off men and women, committing them*
> *to prison"–Acts 8:3-4*

Samaria was one of the most unlikely places Jewish leaders would pursue fleeing Christians. This may have been one reason Philip and others chose Samaria as their new home. When Philip arrived in "the city of Samaria" (probably Shechem), he "preached Christ to them" (Acts 8:5, *NKJV*). These people had been exposed earlier to My ministry by both John the Baptist and My ministry to the Samaritan woman at the well (John 4:1). It is not surprising that the Samaritans were receptive to the gospel as they heard it from Philip.

Philip's preaching was also confirmed by various authenticating signs. Unclean spirits were cast out of the possessed and many lame and other forms of paralysis were miraculously healed. As more people turned to Me, "there was great joy in that city" (Acts 8:8, *NKJV*).

Among those converted in Philip's ministry was a former sorcerer named Simon. He had an ability to make incantations or perform other aspects of occult rituals. But when Philip began performing miracles in Samaria, Simon readily confessed, "This man is the great power of God" (Acts 8:10, *NKJV*). Simon himself converted to Christianity and was baptized by Philip. The conversion of Simon influenced many in the city to reconsider Philip's message and they too came to faith in Me.

Philip's ministry in Samaria was consistent with the intent of the Great Commission to be witnesses "in Samaria" (Acts 1:8, *NKJV*). As news of the new church reached Jerusalem, the apostles visited the city to confirm the new ministry. Philip's ministry among the Samaritans marked a new territory for Christianity. When Peter and John left the Samaritan church to begin their journey back to Jerusalem, they traveled more slowly than they may have normally, "preaching the gospel in many villages of the Samaritans" (Acts 8:25, *NKJV*).

As significant as Philip's ministry was in Samaria, I had something else in store for him. I sent Philip to travel "south along the road which goes down from Jerusalem to Gaza" (Acts 8:26, *NKJV*).

It was only when he arrived that Philip learned the reason for his journey. There he met a prominent Ethiopian official in the government of Queen Candace of Ethiopia. The Ethiopian had traveled to Jerusalem on a religious pilgrimage but left the city with more questions than answers. When Philip found the man reading the scroll of Isaiah, he used the opportunity to explain the gospel to the man. Before long, the Ethiopian trusted Me as Savior and was baptized. According to an early tradition of the Ethiopian Coptic Church, this man then carried the gospel back to his native land and established that church.

After baptizing the Ethiopian and perhaps others in his company, Philip was taken by the Holy Spirit west to the city of Azote, near the Mediterranean Sea. Philip continued his ministry of preaching from town to town, working up the coast until he came to the city of Caesarea. There he apparently settled with his family, although he apparently never abandoned his commitment to sharing the gospel with others. Beginning his lifetime of ministry as a layman, Philip became the only individual in the New Testament called an evangelist (Acts 21:8).

Chapter Six

I AM JESUS:
My Church Expectations

*"The church . . . became stronger as believers lived in fear of
the Lord. And with the encouragement of the Holy Spirit, the
number of churches grew."*

ACTS 9:31, AMPLIFIED

What makes a successful Olympic gold medalist a winner? It is more than training, diet, skills and mastery—it all begins with desire. They want to be exceptional in their field.

What makes a billionaire who has acquired corporations and fortune? It is more than training and knowledge. Each wanted to be exceptional in the financial field.

Who builds a world-class super-church with multitudes in attendance, great finances, influence over mission churches, and influence nationwide or worldwide? It is more than techniques, neighborhoods, opportunity, or super staff. It begins when one determines to be an exceptional follower of Me so that they can evangelize more, teach more, influence more, and build an exceptional church.

The key is to discover God's plan to complete the Great Commission and do it. When I called My followers, I never promised them an easy task, or a "cushy" position, or a big salary, or any of the world's luxuries. I challenged them to win people to Me with gospel preaching and then teach the new converts My belief and way of living. I promise to answer their prayers and use them to change their world. First, they would change their inner world. Second, thay would change the world around them. Finally, they would use their influence to reach and win people in every culture in all the earth.

I am Jesus the Church. When you plant a new church, you are planting My life with new expectations. When you win a person to salvation, I indwell that person's heart (John 14:20). I live in him/her and I shine the light at salvation to their friends and family. When other people are won to salvation, they come together to be a corporate light to shine salvation to others who are lost.

Yes, the church is Me, Jesus! Isn't the church called the body of Christ (Eph. 1:22, 23)? So when you describe the true characteristics of a local church, you're describing My nature. Let me tell you how one man in darkness found the light.

Saul, the religious Pharisee who hated Me, was blinded by My light. Saul had gone through every house in Jerusalem arresting Christians (Acts 8:3) and throwing them in prison. Saul got authority to go to Damascus, to arrest more Christians to bring them back to Jerusalem. As he approached Damascus, I appeared to him in a blinding light; he fell to the ground unable to see. Because he was spiritually blind, I blinded him physically. He cried out, "Who are you, Lord?" (Acts 9:5, *NKJV*). I answered, "I am Jesus, the One you are persecuting!" (Acts 9:5, *NKJV*). Did you see how I shifted the direct object in that sentence? Saul thought he was persecuting Christians, but he actually was persecuting Me. I am Jesus the Church. Because I live in each believer of the church, to persecute them is to persecute Me.

Remember, I promised while teaching on Earth, "For where two or three are gathered together in My name, I am there in the midst of them" (Matt. 18:20, *NKJV*). So when Saul persecuted the Church, he was persecuting Me.

So when you think about growing your church, do not begin planning strategy or organizational techniques. Don't think first of doctrinal statements or even cleaver promotions. And beyond that, a church is not about a denomination, and surely it is not the building, budget or program. A church is an organism; a church is Me, Jesus Christ, in the community.

THE FIRST MENTION OF CHURCH IN SCRIPTURE

A new church is a majestic thing. The first time the word "church" occurs in Scripture, I described it in five words. These words were not deep or theological or mystical. I simply said, "I will build My church" (Matt. 16:18, *NKJV*). I was pointing My disciples to a new entity that I would institute. There was no church in the Old Testament; God the Father had worked through the Jewish nation as His primary plan. There was a king to lead them and prophets to deliver My word to them. And there was a temple in Jerusalem and a priesthood to lead the Jewish nation in worship. But there was nothing as unique as a church.

When I said, "I will build My church," I was looking beyond the cross to a group or assembly of My followers who would carry My message to the entire world. There are five things about the church as seen in My five words of this statement.

"*I* . . ." I am the church builder and I am the church planter. Technically, a church may be planted by a person, couple, or team of people who plant a new church. But I am doing it through them. Because I love all people and want all people to believe in My saving message of the cross, and because it is My purpose to win all nations, I begin each new church.

"*I will* . . ." That word "will" is future tense. I was looking to the future and I wanted you to see My church as the vehicle through which the message of salvation will be preached to the world. The church is not a continuation of the Old Testament but is built on the truth taught in the Old Testament. The Church will become the vehicle through which I will ultimately deliver the message of salvation to lost people.

"*I will build . . .*" The word "build" is continuous action, predicting that I would be continually building My church. What I began in the book of Acts, I will continue throughout the Roman Empire. When the massive Roman Empire collapsed, smaller empires or nations came into existence one after another, and through all those nations, My church continued. Why? Because I am Church, a divine Person. I was empowering My people to live for Me, serve Me, and carry My message to the lost. That was Me preaching to the unsaved. The Church crossed political borders, geographical barriers, cultural and ethnic barriers; all to penetrate the lives of people who believe in Me. And together they became the majestic body of Christ, represented by local churches all over the world.

"*I will build My . . .*" Do you see that possessive pronoun? My Church belongs to Me. Many individuals or groups have claimed possession of the Church. Some call it Presbyterian, some call it Methodist, or Episcopal or Pentecostal. In some places, it does not even have a name; it is just My people assembled together. Some pastors and deacons have referred to it as "my church." But it doesn't belong to one person or group. It does not belong to the official board, the state, or the people. The Church belongs to Me, Jesus Christ.

"*I will build My church . . .*" The word "church" is the Greek word *ecclesia*, which is translated an assembly or gathering of people. My church is a group or assembly of people. In the original language, it is made up of the preposition *ek*, meaning out, and the verb *kalew*, to call. I called My people out from the world. I will call people from self-pursuit, from sin, or anything that would take My place.

But there is a second part to My call: I call people to Myself. When you join a church, you don't just come into a local or denominational Church, but rather you come to Me. You are not just a Baptist or Presbyterian or a member of some local church. I am the church, you belong to Me, and I belong to you (John 14:20). You are called to know Me and make Me known.

THE CHURCH BEGINS WITH JESUS

This book is about My exceptional followers who build exponential churches. These churches are about Me. Why is it imperative I produce exceptional followers, and why exponential churches? The urgency is winning lost people to salvation and that's where it all begins. Technically, everything goes back to Me. Salvation is not primarily about *The Roman Road* to salvation or the *Four Spiritual Laws*; it is as simple as My invitation, "Come unto Me . . ." (Matt. 11:28, *KJV*).

Salvation is coming to Me. This experience is also called believing in Christ, receiving Christ, or following Christ. Didn't I say to some fishermen, "Follow Me, and I will make you fishers of men" (Mark 1:17, *NKJV*)? Didn't I say to Matthew, the tax collector, "Follow Me"? They all did, and their life was transformed.

Everything about My life points to My death on the cross because it was there I died for the sins of the world. Previously, a Jew had to come to the Temple, bringing a sacrificial lamb, where a priest offered it for atonement and forgiveness of sin. But My death changed everything: "Behold! The Lamb of God who takes away the sin of the world!" (John 1:29, *NKJV*). Notice it was not just for the sins of Israel but for the world.

But more importantly than My death is My resurrection. On the third day, I arose from the dead to give new life to those who follow Me. It wasn't enough to have sins forgiven. My followers now have new life—eternal life—which is the life of the Father living in them.

THE GREAT COMMISSION: MY STRATEGY

How was the message of My death and resurrection going to be spread to all the world? I arose early Sunday morning and appeared to a group of women, then later to Peter, Mary Magdalene, and a couple walking home to Emmaus. That evening ten disciples were gathered in the Upper Room for fear of the Jews. Protecting themselves was natural. They thought that since the Jews had executed Me, the Jews were looking to kill them also. The doors were locked. Other than that, the Upper Room was a comfortable place because the disciples had met with Me in the same room for the last supper on Thursday evening.

"Peace be unto you" (John 20:21, *KJV*) was the first thing I said when I appeared to them. Fearful hearts need peace. The last thing I said in that same Upper Room on Thursday evening was "Peace I leave with you, My peace I give to you" (John 14:27, *NKJV*). I gave great words of encouragement.

I showed the disciples the wounds in My hands and side. This was proof that I was the same Jesus. They saw Me and believed. The Bible word for *saw* tells that they touched and examined My wounds carefully. Then I gave them a command of authority and destiny: "As the Father has sent Me, so I am sending you" (John 20:21, *NLT*). I was beginning to give them the Great Commission. This first part was a command to go. Notice what I did not command. I did not tell them where to go, what to do when they got there, nor what to speak—nothing. What I wanted was their unconditional obedience. So I commanded, "Go." Are you willing to obey?

The second giving of the Great Commission occurred a week later. Disciples were again in the Upper Room, except this time there were eleven disciples. Thomas—the doubting disciple—had originally run away farther and hidden deeper than any other disciple. So he was not in the Upper Room that first Sunday evening. But Thomas was now present the second Sunday.

When Thomas finally came out of hiding, the disciples told him they saw Me and touched My wounds. But Thomas always doubted, so he boldly exclaimed, "Except I place my fingers into His wounds, and thrust my fist into His side, I will not believe" (John 20:25, *ELT*). It's terrible to confess you will not believe, but that was evidence of Thomas's doubting heart. I invited Thomas to put his fingers into the wounds of My hands and thrust his fist into My side. Then I added the challenge: "Be not faithless, but believing" (John 20:27, *KJV*).

The Bible does not tell us what Thomas did, but most know he did not accept My invitation to examine My wounds. Instead he fell worshiping Me and exclaimed, "My Lord and my God" (John 20:28, *KJV*). This is the highest of expression of Old Testament deity. Thomas declared that I was not only the Creator God but also the Lord of the universe.

That evening I gave the second aspect of the Great Commission: "Go into all the world and preach the Good News to everyone" (Mark 16:15, *NLT*). Notice carefully, I did not exclude Gentiles, nor did I only include Jews. I said to go everywhere and preach to everyone.

This strategy changed everything. The Father had focused His work on the Jews in the Old Testament; they were His people, and from them would come priests, kings, prophets, the Old Testament, and eventually Me, the Messiah. I had come from the Jews. But this command had a totally new focus. It would take some time for them to understand this expanded command.

The second giving of the Great Commission had an unlimited distinction, "the world," and an unlimited audience, "everyone."

The third giving of the Great Commission was given three or four weeks after My resurrection. The disciples gathered on a mountain in Galilee, near Capernaum. This was the Mount of the Beatitudes. The book of 1 Corinthians describes that there were about 500 people when I appeared on this occasion (1 Cor. 15:6).

This time I included a strategy in the Great Commission: "Go therefore and make disciples of all the nations [*ethne*, people groups] baptizing them . . . teaching them to observe all things that I have commanded you" (Matt. 28:19-20, *NKJV*). This third command included more than a command to announce or preach the gospel to all people. Now I wanted them to get results. Those who heard their preaching would believe, then they were to be baptized, and then they too would be discipled or taught to obey the commands I taught them. Do you see "reproduction" in this command? They were to reach others as they were reached, who in turn would reach others.

These new followers of Mine would come from all ethnic groups or people groups of the world. They would be assembled together in churches by baptism and teaching of the Word of God.

It is interesting that this command instructed, "Make disciples of all people groups." Did I mean to focus on individuals in these ethnic groups so that they would be taught to obey Me? Or did I mean to bring My influence into the culture of these groups so that the gospel would change their culture, or way of life? I meant both!

When I said, "Baptizing them . . .," I meant they were to formally induct new followers into their fellowship. These new believers were to identify with Me—Jesus Christ—spiritually but also identify with them physically in water. These new believers would be identified with the assembly (the church). I was saying to congregationalize all new converts.

By teaching all new converts all things, they would obey what I commanded them. This third giving of the Great Commission suggested they were to preach to lost people, get them saved, then baptize them and gather them into a local assembly for teaching and ministry. This third giving suggested creating a new strategy, i.e., planting reproducing churches. You do that with exponential evangelism and exponential church planting.

The fourth giving of the Great Commission happened 40 days after My death. I and My disciples were in Jerusalem where I clarified the content of the gospel message. They would not instruct followers to come to Jerusalem as the Old Testament commands, nor would they instruct people to bring a sacrificial lamb to the priest for atonement. I taught My disciples to preach My death, burial, and resurrection: "That is how it was written, and that is why it was inevitable that I should suffer, and rise from the dead on the third day. So must the change of heart which leads to the forgiveness of sins be proclaimed in his name to all nations" (Luke 24:46-47, *Phillips*).

My fourth giving of the Great Commission explains the message that must be preached to all ethnic groups in the world. The heart of the gospel message is My death, burial, and resurrection (1 Cor. 15:1-5).

The fifth giving of the Great Commission happened later on that 40th day and it involved geography. The disciples left the city of Jerusalem to walk to the Mount of Olives. They were probably not sure what their commission involved, because they asked, "Will You at this time restore the kingdom?" (Acts 1:6, *NKJV*): "No!" I told them it was not for them to know the times and seasons when the kingdom would be coming. I focused their attention on My original giving of the Great Commission: "You will be My witnesses, telling people about Me everywhere—in Jerusalem, throughout Judea, and Samaria, and to the ends of the earth" (Acts 1:8, *NLT*). This command included geography. They were to begin in Jerusalem, i.e., the city where they were located. When the Great Commission was given to later generations and churches in other locations, they were to begin in their Jerusalem. Each person's Jerusalem is the place where they met Me, prayed, and the Holy Spirit came upon them. From their home base, they are to reach out geographically into the whole world. In each generation and in each different culture, they were to become My exceptional followers who would build exponential churches.

SUMMARY AND CONCLUSION

Why do I have such great expectations of people? Remember, I first created them—they are Mine. Then I loved them enough to die to forgive their sins. Now they are doubly Mine. So I give them great challenges because I believe in them before they believed in Me.

THE GREAT CHALLENGE

Because of My great belief in you,
I ask you to do something greater than you
can do in yourself
Because I know you can get it done.

The challenge to overcome your old nature is great. But you can do it. The command to worship Me only excludes all other options. Then to use your human abilities may seem overwhelming. The task before you may seem greater than any human can do, but I indwell you with My presence. The Holy Spirit will lead you and give you power. The Father will do the miraculous through you. Remember, Paul testified, "I can do all things through Christ who strengthens me" (Phil. 4:13, *NKJV*).

Then I want you to join other followers to get this task done. When you are weak, they may be strong. Fellowship with them, pray with them, work with them, sacrifice with them, but most of all share a common vision of presenting the gospel to every available person, at every available time, using every available resource. When you do that, your church will get exceptional results. But the greatest fact of all—you'll give exponential glory to the Father in heaven.

Chapter Seven

I AM JESUS:
Pictures of My Exponential Church

"I am writing these things to you now ... this is the church of the living God, which is the pillar and foundation of the truth."

1 TIMOTHY 3:14-15, *NLT*

For many centuries humans wanted to fly, but none were successful. Then the Wright brothers figured a way to combine the force of wind to the pull of the Law of Gravity together with the energy and thrust of an engine. They created the airplane and changed the world. When you combine the forces of My church with the energy of dedicated followers who preach the message of salvation, they can change the world.

The answer to world-changing achievements was always there. Its secret was hidden in the elements but not discovered. When humans discovered the secrets, there were scientific and medical breakthroughs.

I put the ingredients of healthy growing churches into the New Testament. Look in the book of Acts and you will see a growing healthy church that created exponential results. It doesn't take a rocket scientist to figure it out. Those were the principles of exceptional church expansions seen in chapter one.

Those foundational principles for growing healthy churches are seen in the 7 faces or pictures in the New Testament. These 7 pictures don't give you practical growth practices. No! They give the picture of growth from their faces. There are different ways to grow, but the bottom line is fruit. Churches have different faces, different names, and different ways to express their worship and outreach. But the bottom line is Me.

When you look at churches today, you see many names, e.g., Baptist, Presbyterian, Lutheran, Episcopal, etc. There are over 3,000 different names. Why so many? Different followers have tried to identify themselves in many different ways. That's alright, but the essence of a church is Me. I am the church. They look at Me through cultural eyes, or organizational eyes, or method eyes, such as one church that emphasizes baptisms or communion.

Then there is another difference among churches. They use many different ways of worshiping or serving Me. Some emphasize liturgy, i.e., organized worship according to their Western culture, episcopal, or orthodox church. Some churches emphasize Bible teaching sermons. They emphasize one major aspect of My commands. Other churches emphasize devotional preaching or motivational sermons to get people to live for Me.

Don't get hung up on the difference. Think of the differences of people. My church is a body, i.e., a person. Just as you expect people to be different, expect churches to be different. Some are beautiful, some are strong, some look intelligent, some act as if they never think. Because I made people different, I made churches different.

I took a normal everyday word—*ecclesia*—to introduce the idea of church to My disciples. *Ecclesia* means "assembly" or "gathering." In its day it meant a political gathering, business gathering, or family gathering. But I had a different idea.

I planned to gather My followers together with a twofold action. First, negative: I would invite them to leave or "repent" and no longer live in the world, i.e., evil practices or principles rebellious to Me.

Instead, they would gather into My assembly to worship Me, learn about Me, serve Me and fellowship together. In the second action, My people would put Me first in their time, talent, and treasures.

I introduced the idea of the church this way: "I will build My church" (Matt. 16:18). I could have used the word "grow," meaning, "I will grow My church." That implied growth by internal forces from the seeds planted. The church would grow that way, but it was more.

I could have said, "I will supervise My church." That would suggest My outward energy to do it all.

I could have said, "I will expand . . ." That would suggest a business model and would have focused only on what the church had to offer.

Also, I didn't say, "I will organize . . ." That would have emphasized outward things like programs, services, and committees.

But I said, "I will build My church." The word "build" is in the active voice; I will continually build My church. That involves all the above actions. I will plant the church and let it grow according to the energy of the seed of the gospel. Some churches will be worshiping churches, others will be Bible study churches, and others will be evangelistic churches. Some will be churches emphasizing small groups, or churches emphasizing ministry, or churches emphasizing healing and restoration. I wanted it to be all those things. I would be its source of life, energy, and direction. All spiritual energy would come from Me. When I used the phrase "build My church," I was describing both outward energy from Me and inward energy through the members in that church. The church would grow both an organism and organization. It would not only grow like My human body but would grow like a God-made organization.

But notice the possessive pronoun "My"; the church will belong to Me. I will be its inner life and vitality; I will be its organization and management. I will be the force that motivates you in the morning to meet Me and talk with Me. Then I will minister throughout the day.

The church will be Me.

I gave 7 descriptions of My church in Scripture. Each of the following 7 descriptive "faces" will emphasize a different strength or function of My church. I knew the world had all kinds of cultures, so I knew My church had to look different in different cultures. I don't describe these cultures, but I manifest Myself in different ways in each culture.

7 FACES OF THE CHURCH

PICTURE	CENTRAL TRUTH
1. Body	1. Unity in life and function
2. Building	2. My indwelling
3. Bride	3. Intimacy with Me
4. Flock	4. Provision, I care for each
5. Garden (vine)	5. Growth and fruit
6. Family	6. Relationship
7. Priesthood	7. Service

Remember, no two people on Earth look alike. Just as people are different, so too churches will have different appearances, functions, and natures. Rather than describing doctrines or practices that are not church (negative), I give 7 descriptions or faces so you can compare churches you see in the everyday world to what I think a church should look like. You are looking at pictures or faces of My assembly of believers on this earth.

1. *My church is described as a body*. Paul tells you that gifts are given to leadership to build up the church, the body of Christ (Eph. 4:12). This picture shows My church growing like a physical body grows. I am Jesus, the head of My body; the church is people, or My followers (Eph. 4:12).

What does a head do to the body? Bob Saucy in his *Theology of the Local Church* says, "There are six aspects or principles how I the head of the church relate to My body: 1. Unity, 2. Diversity, 3. Mutuality, 4. Sovereign leadership, 5. Source of life, 6. Sustenance of life."[3]

Every Christian should give Me first place in everything in their life, just as every church must realize I am its head and I must have first place in each church. Why? Because "Everything was created through Me and for Me" (Col. 1:16, *NKJV*), "I existed before anything else" (Col. 1:17, *NLT*), and "I hold all creation together" (Col. 1:17). As a result, I must be first (preeminent) in all things (Col. 1:18).

That means that when a church body is healthy, all its parts should function properly and carry out My will, its head. When disease and sickness strike the body, usually it attacks the greatest weakness in the body and incapacitates the whole body. And that happens in local churches when individuals sin or when someone in leadership violates My commandments. The whole body is disabled (1 Cor. 12:26). I describe the church as a body to teach that you need one another, should care for one another, love another, and grow together in Me.

2. My church is described as the temple of God. My church is described as a growing temple edifice. Paul told the Ephesians, "Together, we are his house, built on the foundation of the apostles and the prophets. And the cornerstone is Christ Jesus Himself. We are carefully joined together in him, becoming a holy temple for the Lord. Through him you Gentiles are also being made part of this dwelling where God lives by his Spirit" (Eph. 2:20-22, *NLT*).

Remember, each individual believer's body is the temple of the Holy Spirit (1 Cor. 3:16; 2 Cor. 6:19). Therefore, every believer's body is indwelt by the Holy Spirit. When believers come together corporately, the Holy Spirit indwells each of them and He indwells the corporate community: "Don't you realize that all of you together are the temple of God and that the Spirit of God lives in you?" (1 Cor. 3:16, *NLT*).

Just as believers grow in grace and maturity, so to the local church should grow in mutual ability to serve, becoming more mature and more effective in My ministry. Do you see the picture of growth? Both believers and their local assembly are growing at the same time.

In the Old Testament Israel worshiped first in a tent called the tabernacle and second in a temple where the Father, Son and Holy Spirit came to reside. We entered the temple as a Shekinah Glory cloud (Exod. 40:34; 2 Chron. 5:13, 14). We were pleased to dwell among Our people. The Bible describes Moses putting the tabernacle together exactly as We commanded him in Exodus 40. That involves setting up the walls of the tabernacle, putting furniture in its place, and placing the Ark of the Covenant in the Holy of Holies: "Then the cloud covered the tabernacle, and the glory of the Lord filled the tabernacle" (Exod. 40:34, *NLT*). What a magnificent sight, that We dwelt among Our people. Today, We dwell in My church as it is an assembly of My people when the church is described as a temple.

Remember, a temple has three sections: the first, the foundation; the second, the cornerstone; and finally the building blocks of stones of which the building is made. Bob Saucy said, "The apostles have laid the foundations by teaching the doctrines of Christ and bringing men into a relationship with him who is the only foundation that is laid. The church is not built upon a man or creed, but upon the person of the living Christ."[4]

The fact that the church is a temple exhorts you to live holy. Paul said, "But let every man take heed how he buildeth thereupon . . . . If any man build upon the foundation . . . every man's work . . . who is a living stone in the building can also be a builder of the building" (1 Cor. 3:10, 12, 13, *KJV*).

3. *My church is described as a bride.* John invites the readers of Revelation, "Come, I will show you the bride, the Lamb's wife" (Rev. 21:9, *NKJV*). Paul expounded this truth when he said, "For I am jealous for you with the jealousy . . . I promised you as a pure bride to one husband—Christ" (2 Cor. 11:2, *NLT*), "For the husband is head

of the wife, as also Christ is head of the church; and He is the Savior of the body. Therefore, just as the church is subject to Christ, so let the wives be to their own husbands in everything. Husbands, love your wives, just as Christ also loved the church and gave Himself for her, that He might sanctify and cleanse her with the washing of water by the word, that He might present her to Himself a glorious church, not having spot or wrinkle or any such thing, but that she should be holy and without blemish. So husbands ought to love their own wives as their own bodies; he who loves his wife loves himself. For no one ever hated his own flesh, but nourishes and cherishes it, just as the Lord does the church. For we are members of His body, of His flesh and of His bones. For this reason a man shall leave his father and mother and be joined to his wife, and the two shall become one flesh. This is a great mystery, but I speak concerning Christ and the church" (Eph. 5:23-32, *NKJV*). The main truth about My bride is our intimacy and love for each other. Why should you love Me with all your heart? Because I first loved you completely and without measure.

You must learn of My love for every church member and for the church corporately so that you "may be able to comprehend with all the saints, what *is* the width and length and depth and height—to know the love of Christ which passes knowledge" (Eph. 3:18, 19, *NKJV*). When you understand how much I love you, then you're able to respond in love to Me with all your heart. Since I have given everything to you, you must give everything back to Me. And remember that the nature of love is giving; just as a bride gives herself to her husband, so too you must give yourself to Me, and serve Me through the church.

4. *My church is described as the flock of God.* When Paul met with the elders in Ephesus, he challenged them, "Therefore take heed to yourselves and to all the flock, among which the Holy Spirit has made you overseers, to shepherd the church of God which He purchased with His own blood" (Acts 20:28, *NKJV*). The local church is like a flock of sheep.

The greatness of Psalm 23 shows My shepherd care over My sheep followers. When you come into My church, I am the Shepherd who oversees you, My sheep in My fold.

Remember, the word "pastor" comes from *poimen,* which means shepherd. So, the pastor of a local church is a shepherd of souls. Technically, they are the under-shepherd under Me, I am Shepherd of the flock of God.

There is a difference between flock and fold. I noted this difference: "I have other sheep, too, that are not in this sheep fold. I must bring them also. They will listen to My voice, and there will be one flock with one shepherd" (John 10:16, *NLT*).

I am using two different words to describe a gathering of believers. First is the *fold,* which describes the outward organization, and the second is *flock,* which describes the inner unity of the sheep in Me. Overall you can liken this picture to be the *organizational* church as opposed to the *organic* church.[5]

Since I am the chief Shepherd, when I appear in the Second Coming, I will reward My faithful under-shepherds (1 Pet. 5:4).

Donald McGavran says that the Great Commission is fulfilled by finding sheep (evangelism), folding sheep (baptizing), and feeding sheep (discipling or teaching). He goes on to say, "God wants countable lost persons found. The shepherd with 99 lost sheep who stays at home feeding or caring for them should not expect commendation. God will not be pleased by the excuse that His servant was doing something 'more spiritual than searching for stray sheep.' Nothing is more spiritual than the natural reconciliation of the lost to God."[6]

5. *My church is described as a garden.* A local church is reflective of a collection of several organic growing entities, i.e., fields, vines, plantings, farm, husbandry, and fruit trees.

A garden is a cultivated plot of ground where weeds and rocks are removed, seed is sown and can be cared for until grown. Then crops and fruit are harvested.

What does the description of the church as a garden tell you? Each Christian must depend upon Me alone as the only source of life, growth, and harvest. This is what I meant when I said, "Abide in Me, and I in you. As the branch cannot bear fruit of itself, unless it abides in the vine, neither can you, unless you abide in Me" (John 15:4, *NKJV*).

Did you see the double transference in that description? First, I am in (indwell) the believer when I say, "I in you." That is My indwelling or the source of power. The second transference is "You in Me," which is your union with Me. Paul calls this "in Christ" in the heavenlies. You must be attached to Me to get spiritual life, growth, and produce a harvest. This implies prayer, study of the Word, meditation, and yieldedness to Me. Both the vine (Me) and branches (Christians) make up the church, but spiritual power or fruit only flows one way. It comes from Me to the believer.

Remember, the purpose of the garden is fruit bearing. And what is fruit? First, it is winning souls. Just as a fig tree produces figs, and a grape vine produces grapes, so too you as a Christian should lead another person to faith in Me.

But fruit bearing is also your inner character, described as the fruit of the Spirit (singular). Paul describes, "But the Holy Spirit produces this kind of fruit in our lives: love, joy, peace, patience, kindness, goodness, faithfulness, gentleness, and self-control" (Gal. 5:22, 23, *NLT*). And what is character? It is habitually doing the right thing, at the right time, for the right purpose.

Don't forget that I said the Father must prune the branches for a harvest to continue: "I am the true grapevine, and my Father is the gardener. He cuts off every branch of mine that doesn't produce fruit, and he prunes the branches that do bear fruit so they will produce even more" (John 15:1, 2, *NLT*). This means you can grow in all ways and you must produce fruit.

Many things happen in a local church that hinder growth: sometimes false doctrine, sin, unyieldedness, and self-will. But I prune the branches (Christians) in My church to cut out things that strangle growth and cut off fruit. The entire purpose is that the church will win souls and grow strong mature followers so too the vine (church) will produce a harvest.

6. *My church is described as a family of God.* There are several pictures in the New Testament that describe Christians: children, sons, daughters, saints, sanctified ones, believers, disciples, brethren, sisters, and of course, family. And the Christian family comes together under God the Father. All these terms reflect relationship in a local church.

John describes how believers become the Father's children when they believe in Me: "But to all who believed him and accepted him, he gave the right to become children of God" (John 1:12, *NLT*). What do I say about them? They are born again (John 1:13). In another place I describe being born into the Father's family: "You must be born again" (John 3:7, *NLT*).

The church is a family, God is your Father in heaven, and I am the body; the Holy Spirit works to build it up and use it in ministry. Believers call one another brothers and sisters, as they relate to one another in the family of God.

7. *My church is described as a priesthood.* In the Old Testament, a Levite was set aside to the office of priesthood to serve the Godhead. When the church is described as a priesthood, it focuses attention on your serving Us. Technically, I, Christ, am the Priest for all believers. Paul reminds us, "There is one God and one Mediator who can reconcile God and humanity—the man Christ Jesus" (1 Tim. 2:5, *NLT*). I am the ultimate Priest, but I have given you a ministry of priesthood: you serve or minister in the task you perform, then you offer praise or worship, and finally you pray or intercede for My entire ministry through My church on Earth.

The Old Testament priesthood reflected these threefold functions. First, they sacrificed animals for the people, leading to the forgiveness of sins. Second, they led people in worship to God.

Third, they made intercession for individuals with their fasting and prayers.

As priests, one of your main functions is worship: "Therefore, let us offer through Jesus a continual sacrifice of praise to God, proclaiming our allegiance to his name" (Heb. 13:15, *NLT*).

SUMMARY AND CONCLUSION

At one time, identifying a church was simple. It was a group of believers meeting to fellowship with Me, to learn about Me, and carry out My Great Commission. That concept of the church was stretched when believers constructed a building and met under its roof. They called this structure a church and in its rooms or auditorium they carried out My ministry as a church. As adequate as that definition of church was, it didn't quite include all the functions or faces of the New Testament.

Today, there are new ways to compose a church.

Is a church known by its existence or by its purpose? Just because a group of believers call themselves a church does not necessarily mean they are a church. I may bless them, use them, and even manifest My presence in them. Because their intent is noble, and the ministry they do is biblical, are you worthy to deny them the name of church?

However, groups that are identified as a church in the New Testament became a model for ministry and were blessed when I manifested Myself in them.

Remember, the Bible is not a written theology book. There are many expressions of systematic theology written by men such as Calvin, Hodge, Strong, and Chafer. Also, there are corporate expressions of systematic theology as in the Nicene Creed, the Chalcedonian Creed, the Westminster Confession of Faith, and the New Hampshire Statement of Faith (used by early Baptists in America). In these works there are both limitations and extensions as they try to define or describe a church.

The New Testament is not a theological textbook, but rather it reflects how people communicated with Me, their Lord, and the Father and Holy Spirit. My followers lived in Us, worshiped Us, and served Us. Try to understand the church in this reflection.

The Scriptures are a revelation of Our nature and purpose, so from the Bible you can know Us better and understand what My church ought to look like and how it should minister.

You understood that when church people assemble together—in a church—that assembly would look differently in different cultures. It would feel different when dominated by different age groups, different cultures, and different socio-economic levels of society. We created every person different, but at the same time We use each person according to their strengths and the spiritual gifts given them. Perhaps We wanted churches to be different in feeling, expression, and emphasis, yet cut from the same pattern so each would have similar characteristics, i.e., My characteristics.

My church is like a person, and I created each person to be in-dependent-dependent. They are independent before Me and stand alone in accountability to Me. That means they only answer to Me. But yet each person is dependent on Me for their life, purpose, and function. Also each person is dependent on other people for social life, mental growth, emotional happiness, and spiritual fellowship. These two forces operate at times against each other and at other times in cooperation with each other.

The independence of humans indicates they must direct their own life and be responsible for everything they do. It's the same for a church. But in isolation the individuals realize they can only find meaning and purpose in connection with others. Again, it's the same for the church. Because what you want and need cannot be acquired by just yourself, you must communicate with and depend upon oth-er people to help you find the basic necessities of life. These include food, clothing, shelter, and emotional happiness. Your dependence need is satisfied in Me, the church.

So, just as a person is independent, so every local church as a body is independent of all other churches and must find its doctrinal stability in the Word of God. It finds its practice of Christian living from Me and in the final analysis, will be accountable to Me. But every church must relate to all other churches in mutual fellowship and mutual support. Every church must demonstrate that they are one in My body with other churches and that every believer is one with all other believers. They must be one in purpose, one in passion, and one in shared values.

All believers can't be in one church, but each believer can be loyal to his/her church, serve in that church and, from that church, reach out to complete My Great Commission.

NOTES

1. Jerry Falwell, *Capturing a Town for Christ* (Old Tappan, NJ: Fleming H. Revell Company, 1973), 84.
2. Rick Warren, *A Purpose-Driven Church* (Grand Rapids, MI: Zondervan, 1995).
3. Robert Saucy, *The Church in God's Program* (Chicago, IL: Moody Press, 1972), 26.
4. Ibid., 33-34.
5. Ibid., 46.
6. Donald A. McGavran, *Understanding Church Growth* (Grand Rapids, MI: Wm. B. Eerdmans, 1970), 4.

PART TWO

Lets
Talk
50 Daily Devotionals

ollow Me. I am Jesus. When you follow Me with all your heart, mind, soul and body, you will become an exceptional Christian. What does the word *exceptional* mean? It means you are extraordinary, or remarkable, or unexpected. I want to make you an outstanding believer. That is what I do; I asked fishermen to follow Me and they became fishers of people—evangelists—who won multitudes to salvation. Think of Peter's preaching at Pentecost; over 3,000 were added to the church (Acts 3:4), and after his next sermon there were 5,000 men added to the church (Acts 4:4). That meant family heads were added to the church, including their wives and children. Some have estimated over 20,000 followers.

They became exceptional followers; you can become an exceptional follower also. What must you do? Talk to Me in prayer in the next 50 days. First, I will explain the Scriptures to you and how you can become exceptional. Then you will tell Me your needs and desires. We will have a conversation—talking to each other. You can become far more exceptional than you ever dreamed.

That doesn't mean you will be perfect, but you can become an exceptional worshiper; that is where it all begins. Then you will become an exceptional intercessor, asking Me to do extraordinary works through you. Then you will become an exceptional witness to both the saved and the lost. The results can be extraordinary.

When you follow Me, you will be baptized into a local body of Christ called the local church. You can influence them as they influence you. Together with them, your church can have exponential results. The word *exponential* means the church is a living, growing body rapidly increasing in all areas according to a predetermined formula.

What's an exponential church? Its formula is motivated by My Great Commission, charged with preaching the gospel to everyone in the world. Will you help Me do that? The next 50 days of devotions will illustrate how the original Jerusalem church grew exponentially in every area. It saturated its city, then the surrounding area of Judea. Next it reached out to Samaria, a culture different from its own.

Then My church in Antioch sent out missionaries until the entire Roman Empire was saturated with the gospel. Now I want you to join in that crusade. I want you and all My followers in your church to become exponential witnesses.

Each of the next 7 weeks is divided into 7 daily devotions. The devotions for each week will help you and your church to become exceptional in character so that your church will become exponential in method and service.

WEEK 1 | I Am Jesus—A Church Growing Exponentially

WEEK 2 | I Am Jesus—A Revived Church

WEEK 3 | I Am Jesus—A Witnessing Church

WEEK 4 | I Am Jesus—A Teaching Church

WEEK 5 | I Am Jesus—A Ministering and Serving Church

WEEK 6 | I Am Jesus—My Church Expectations

WEEK 7 | I Am Jesus—Pictures of My Exponential Church

WEEK ONE

I AM JESUS:
A Church Growing Exponentially

The New Testament church is vastly different from the Old Testament sacrificial system and Jewish laws. The church was new, refreshing, freeing, and God the Father placed the life of the Holy Spirit in it. But most important, the church is Me, the body of Christ. I am Jesus living in My people and touching the world through My people. This week your reading and praying will focus on what I do for My people and for My church. When you properly know Me, you will strive to become an exceptional follower. What are the results? Many exceptional followers can build an exponential church.

I AM JESUS—*Be an Exceptional Believer*

"But you will receive power when the Holy Spirit comes upon you. And you will be my witnesses, telling people about me everywhere—in Jerusalem, throughout Judea, in Samaria, and to the ends of the earth."

ACTS 1:8, *NLT*

I am Jesus who calls you to a life of exceptional character. The word *exceptional* means you are extraordinary, remarkable, and unexpected. Don't live the way you lived before you began following Me. Reach higher, become more than you ever thought you could become: "If any person is in Me, they are a new creature" (2 Cor. 5:17, *BBJ*). I want to create you to be a remarkable worshiper, so you worship the Father in spirit (Holy Spirit) and truth (scripture). I want you to become a remarkable testimony to the saved and lost. When they look at you, I want them to see Me and be drawn to salvation. I want you to grow extraordinary faith—faith to move mountains (Mark 11:22-24). I want you to believe that I exist (Heb. 11:6), and that I will do remarkable ministries through you.

Lord, in my flesh I see my weaknesses and failures. Fill me with Your presence, give me a burden for ministry, direct me to the place You choose for me to serve. Then use me. Amen.

I am Jesus, who wants you and your church to be exceptional. Then you will see exponential results. The word *exponential* means explosion of growth according to My Great Commission. If you are exceptional in character, then I will use you in exponential ways. So learn, grow, worship, serve, and follow Me all the way, every day.

I have decided to follow You. I will be what you want me to be. I will go where You want me to go. I will do what You tell me to do. My commitment is for all my life, for all the days of my life. Amen.

READING: Acts 8:1-40

KEY THOUGHT: I want you to be My exceptional follower, so I can do exceptional ministry through you.

I AM JESUS—*Be an Exponential Church*

"But you will receive power when the Holy Spirit comes upon you.
And you will be my witnesses, telling people about me everywhere—in Jerusalem,
throughout Judea, in Samaria, and to the ends of the earth."

ACTS 1:8, NLT

My church should be *exponential* in every way. The word exponential means rapid increase in all areas according to a predetermined formula. I gave the Great Commission as a predetermined strategy to get the gospel to all lost people. The power to get it done is in the Holy Spirit. The motive is love—I love all lost people: "The love of Christ constrains (you) . . . because (I) died for all" (2 Cor. 5:14-15, ELT). Also remember I said, "The works that I do (you) shall do also, and greater works" (John 14:12). What is greater than physical healing and turning 5 loaves and 2 fish into enough to feed 5,000? I tell you—its winning one hell-bound sinner to salvation, or even better, winning a whole church to salvation and getting them exponentially aggressive to reach their neighborhood—then planting another church in another unevangelized area.

Lord, forgive my sinful negligence. I will get serious about sharing my faith with family and friends. Help me see their lost condition and give me a boldness to win them to salvation. Amen.

Exponential means increased effort motivated by the Holy Spirit. The bottom line is not just a foreign missions program, or techniques, or methods. It is being personally energized to exponential fasting and prayer. That will lead to exponential giving that will led to exponential evangelism that results in exponential blessings. What's another word for exponential? Revival! Revival is My pouring My presence on My people. Do you need reviving?

Lord, revive my spirit. I pray but need more fervency.
I serve but need more fruitfulness. Drops of mercy are falling around me,
but I ask for revival showers. Amen.

READING: Mark 16:14-20; Acts 1:1-11

KEY THOUGHT: The greatness of the Great Commission demands our total commitment and energy to complete the task.

Day 3

I AM JESUS—*A Church Praying*

"Stay here in the city until the Holy Spirit comes and fills you with power."
LUKE 24:49, *NLT*

"Then they all prayed . . . all the believers were meeting together in one place,
suddenly . . . everyone present was filled with the Holy Spirit."
ACTS 1:24; 2:1, 4

I am Jesus the church gathered for prayer—exponential prayer. Not just another group prayer meeting, but a time of confessing sin, admitting your failures, begging for spiritual power and faith to believe the Holy Spirit will come to fill with zeal and soul-winning evangelism. The early church prayed with boldness (Acts 4:29), and the room was shaken. Ultimately they were accused of "turning the world upside down" (Acts 17:6). What does that mean? The gospel transforms people and they changed their life and family. When that is added to a whole church, a neighborhood is turned upside down. Do you believe the church can change the world? Since I indwell a person (Gal. 2:20), let Me shine through you into your family and world.

Fill me with the Holy Spirit and revive me, so my testimony can revive my church
and change my world. Amen.

I am Jesus who promised "if you ask anything in My name, I will do it" (John 14:14, *NKJV*). So what is on your prayer list? Are you praying for lost family members to be saved? Have you prayed for opportunities to witness to them, to get them under the gospel preaching? Everything in your walk with Me begins with prayer. First, pray to know Me. Then pray to be filled with great faith; and third, pray to be an aggressive soul winner. Ask for revival in your church—then people will get saved: "You do not have because you do not ask" (Jas. 4:2, *NKJV*).

Lord, teach me to pray with bigger faith to expect You to do more in my family
and church. Teach me to pray for bigger results in evangelism. Lord, give me a
bigger burden to worship and serve You in all I do. Amen.

READING: Acts 4:1-31

KEY THOUGHT: The Great Commission expects great results in your church, so you and all in the church must give yourselves to great prayer.

I AM JESUS—*Exponential Faith*

"Jesus said to them . . . 'If you had faith even as small as a mustard seed,
you could say to this mountain, move from here to there, and it would move.
This happens only with prayer and fasting.'"

MATTHEW 17:20-21, ELT

I am Jesus, the Church body (Eph. 1:22-23). When two or three come together for prayer, I am in your midst (Matt. 18:20). Because I indwell you and all other saved people in your church, I want you to do exponential things for gospel outreach. Do you have obstacles? Are there mountains that stop you from going forward? Ask for faith to move mountains. You move problems first on your knees before you move them with your hands and head. Fast for God to remove obstacles, and pray for God to fill you with power for exponential outreach in evangelism. I am still alive, and the Holy Spirit is still available, ask for great spiritual breakthroughs in your church outreach: "According to your faith let it be to you" (Matt. 9:29, *NKJV*).

Lord, I want You to begin a revival in my heart. I need Your blessing and
power before I can touch the lives of others. Give me faith to believe You for
greater things and give me the boldness to witness for You. Fill me with the
Spirit and use me. Amen.

I am Jesus who grows churches (Eph. 4:16). Just as children grow when they have a proper diet and exercise, so to your church should be growing. Does it have a healthy diet of scripture teaching? Is it exercising evangelism to the lost? Everything in your Christian life begins in prayer, like the early church prayed and God increased their reach into the lost community. So let's pray, believe, work, and evangelize.

Lord, give me faith to obey the Great Commission.
Give me a burden to pray for lost people to get saved. Give me opportunities
to witness. Now give me boldness to do it. Amen.

READING: Hebrews 11:1-40

KEY THOUGHT: There must be great faith by leaders and people to solve problems and work to reach the community with the gospel.

Day 5

I AM JESUS—*Exponential Praying*

"I will pour out My Spirit upon all people."
JOEL 2:29, NLT

"Suddenly, there was a sound from heaven like the roaring of a mighty windstorm . . . it filled the house . . . everyone was filled with the Holy Spirit."
ACTS 2:2, 4, NLT

I am Jesus who poured out the Holy Spirit on 120 believers on the Day of Pentecost. It didn't happen just because I promised to do it. It happened because they fasted and prayed and prepared to obey the Great Commission. They fasted and prayed for 50 days. That is a long time to continue praying and worshiping without seeing results. How long will you worship, and wait, and pray, to become an exponential church that will change the world? Remember, because they had the power of the Holy Spirit, it was said, "These that have turned the world upside down are come here also" (Acts 17:5, ELT). To get exponential results, you must be an exceptional follower. Go stand under the spigot, pray and wait for Me to fill you.

Lord, I want to change my world. I want to worship and pray exponentially. I want to testify and serve exponentially. I want to see exponential results in my church. Use me to begin. Amen.

I am Jesus who will make you an exceptional follower. If you let Me pour out the Holy Spirit on you, you can see exponential results in your prayer life, your Bible study, your ministry and your worship. Are you satisfied with the old life you lived before I came into your life? Begin by being filled with the Spirit. Stand, wait, pray, and believe.

Lord, I don't want a self-centered life like people in the world. I want to be Christ-centered. I want You to control my life. Control my thoughts . . . my desires . . . my work . . . and my leisure activities. I yield to You fully. Amen.

READING: Acts 12:5-19

KEY THOUGHT: When believers in a church seek the fullness of the Holy Spirit and let Him control their life and ministry, the church will have exponential blessings.

I AM JESUS—*Exponential Blessings*

"Those who believe . . . were baptized and added to the church . . . about 3000 in all."

ACTS 2:41, *NLT*

"All believers devoted themselves to . . . teaching . . . fellowship . . . sharing meals . . . prayer . . . worshiped together . . . and met in homes for the Lord's Supper."

ACTS 2:42, *NLT*

I am Jesus who poured exponential blessings on the new church. Those blessings were rapidly displayed in the church. They enjoyed My presence in their gatherings and they worshiped new and differently. They did not bring their animal sacrifices to the brazen altar. I was the Lamb slain to take away sins (John 1:29). They worshiped in their homes, and the streets belonged to the church to preach, testify, and serve. They went everywhere witnessing for Me. They experienced blessings never felt in the Old Testament. I had forgiven their sins, had indwelt their life, and had given them confidence and assurance never before realized. They were ministering directly for Me, not for the priest or temple. This was the age of the church—My presence in them. This was the age of the Holy Spirit—with exponential blessings.

> *Lord, I admit my faith is sometimes dull and uninspiring. I don't trust You for miracles, and I don't expect exponential blessings in my life. Forgive my sins, revive my spirit, and give me a new vision of how I can serve You and receive exponential blessings. Amen.*

I am Jesus who gives exponential blessings to those who seek to do My perfect will for their life (Rom. 12:1). I will fill those with the Holy Spirit who seek and are yielded to Me (1 Cor. 3:16, Eph. 5:18). I will pour out exponential blessings on those who follow Me with exceptional faith.

> *Lord, I want more in my life than I now have. I want Your presence to fill me with joy so I can worship You with honesty. I want You to give me power in service so I can do exponential ministry for You. I wait for Your presence. Amen.*

READING: Galatians 5:16-25

KEY THOUGHT: I will give exponential blessings to those who put Me first in their life and seek to serve Me with their entire life.

I AM JESUS—*Less Than Exponential*

"Write this letter to . . . the church in Laodicea . . . I know all the things you do,
that you are neither hot nor cold. I wish that you were one or the other!
But since you are like lukewarm water, neither hot nor cold,
I will spit you out of my mouth!"

REV. 3:14-16, NLT

I am the church of all types of believers—some who have grown in their faith, others who are carnal, even babies in Christ (1 Cor. 3:1). Therefore, not all churches have a strong exponential outreach. Letters were written to the 7 churches (Rev. 2–3). One left its first love of evangelism (Rev. 2:5), another was ignorant of doctrine and fell into error (Rev. 2:12-17), and another had members living in sin and immorality (Rev. 2:18-20). There were other problems, so I challenged them, "repent and do the first works" (Rev. 2:5, *NKJV*). Actually the spiritually of churches is a reflection of the spirituality of its members. How spiritual is your church or its members? What must you do personally to have revival and become My exceptional followers?

> *Lord, sometimes I am blind to sin in my life (ignorant sin). Open my*
> *eyes to see anything that is holding me back. My problem is, I don't yield*
> *enough to You and I don't pursue godliness. Make me an exceptional*
> *follower so that my church will express exceptional evangelism and*
> *growth. Amen.*

I indwell all believers, but not everyone is a shining testimony to the gospel light. Some have not tried to grow in their faith; others have given into temptation and sinned against Me. Sin blinds their spiritual eyes so they don't know what they do, nor do they know how blind they are to Me.

> *Lord, forgive my sin, cleanse me and make me usable. Fill me with the*
> *Holy Spirit to serve You effectively. Make me an exceptional follower.*
> *I want to be a member of an exponential church. Amen.*

READING: Revelation 2:1-29

KEY THOUGHT: I want every follower to be an exceptional Christian, but they are not. I want every church to be an exponential church, but it isn't.

WEEK TWO

I AM JESUS:
A Church Revived

The key to exponential growth is revival strength from the Holy Spirit. God the Father promised, "I will pour out My Spirit." The pouring began at Pentecost and continues today. This week read how to begin a revival in your church and keep it going. The secret of a great exponential church is not with God but begins with you and your church. Revival is defined as "God pouring His presence on His people." To have the Holy Spirit poured on you, you must desire it, seek it, pray for it, and receive it when it comes. Don't you want the Father's presence? Don't you want revival? What is the secret? Go stand under the spout to find out.

I AM JESUS—*A Church Revived*

"I will pour out My Spirit on all flesh."
JOEL 2:28, *NLT*

"Everyone was filled with the Holy Spirit."
ACTS 2:4, *NLT*

I am Jesus looking for My church to be revived. And what is revival? It is God pouring His presence on His people. That occurred on the Day of Pentecost, and I can revive your church. To get revived, you and the other members of your church must wait in prayer. What do you think they were doing as they waited for Pentecost? How do you think they prayed? They confessed and begged for My presence, they interceded for their lost friends and family, they worshiped, they fasted! Wrapped up in their intercession was sacrifice. It takes sacrifice to get the full blessings of God. You must empty out self and fill your life with My presence.

Lord, I need revival. Motivate my heart to seek revival. I have hidden sin there (ignorant sin); cleanse me and point me to Your cross. Help me sacrifice as You did on the cross. Send revival to my church and do it through me. Amen.

I am Jesus, wanting to revive your church. Yes, I want to give you joy and blessings, but most of all, I want to evangelize lost people in your neighborhood. I want you to go get them saved, then baptize them and put them into ministry, helping you do the work of evangelism. I want My house filled.

Lord, forgive me for only looking at my needs and my problems. Give me eyes to see Your church and help me revive it. Use me in evangelism to reach the lost around me. Amen.

READING: Luke 14:16-35

KEY THOUGHT: Churches that are not exponential in outreach need to be revived. I need to pour the Holy Spirit on them.

Day 9

I AM JESUS—A *Spirit-filled Church*

"Don't be drunk with wine, because that will ruin your life.
Instead, be filled with the Holy Spirit."

EPH. 5:18, *NLT*

You as a believer can be filled with the Holy Spirit. When you and others in your church are filled with the Spirit, you become an awesome tool. When Paul and Barnabas took the gospel to Antioch in Turkey, many were saved in the Jewish synagogue (Acts 12:14-52). The unbelieving Jews attacked the new Gentile believers because they were filled with envy (13:45). But "the word of the Lord was published throughout the region because the believers were filled with joy and with the Holy Spirit" (Acts 13:49, ELT). When they were filled with the Holy Spirit, exponential aggressive evangelism resulted. Perhaps you or your church have not experienced evangelism because you are not Holy Spirit filled (Luke 14:23).

Lord, I am empty; fill me with the Holy Spirit. I am not accomplishing much
for Your kingdom; fill me with the Holy Spirit. I want to be an effective witness
for You and I want my church to grow. Amen.

To be filled with the Holy Spirit first you must empty yourself of sin and pride. I won't fill dirty vessels. Next, you must ask the Holy Spirit to fill your thoughts, desires and relationships. I won't go where I am not welcome. The third step is filling your life with the Word of God. The Bible will control your thoughts, desires and actions. The filling of the Holy Spirit and scriptures go hand in hand. You won't get one without the other. So, the first step begins with you.

Lord, I want to be used in aggressive evangelism—fill me with the Spirit. I will read,
memorize and meditate on Your Word; let it control my life. I ask You now, start
filling me with the Holy Spirit, and don't stop till I am filled up to the brim. Amen.

READING: Acts 13:14-52

KEY THOUGHT: The Holy Spirit is available and wants to fill you, but it begins with your wanting Him and asking Him to fill you.

I AM JESUS—*Sender of the Holy Spirit*

"I will ask the Father and He will give you ... the Holy Spirit, who leads into all truth."
JOHN 14:16, *NLT*

I will send the Holy Spirit to do many things for you. He will convict (cause to see) your sin (John 16:8). He will show you biblical truth (John 14:26). He will fill you with authority to do ministry (Eph. 5:18). He will give you authority in ministry so that lost people are saved and believers grow. He will guide you in daily living (Gal. 5:18). He will build Christian character in your life, called the fruit of the Spirit (Gal. 5:22-23). He has energy to motivate you to repentance,   to deeper prayers, and to exponential evangelism. Don't try to serve the heavenly Father on your own or out of habit. Ask the Holy Spirit to fill you and use you.

> *Lord, I need a fresh touch from Your presence. Lately I haven't been
> productive in Your ministry. Fill me with the Holy Spirit. I yield to You
> and seek Your power in my life. Amen.*

The Holy Spirit won't come to exalt Himself (John 16:13). He will quietly exalt Me in your life (Phil. 1:27) and will lead you in "Spirit worship" of the Father (John 4:23-24). He will give you authority and power in ministry (Acts 1:8). Don't you need the Holy Spirit today to help you succeed in your ministry and Christian living? If your life has fallen into a daily routine, ask the Holy Spirit to fill you and use you.

> *Holy Spirit, come revive my vision of serving and living for the Father.
> Come revive my ministry for Jesus. Come, Holy Spirit, give me inner joy and
> confidence in all I do for You. Amen.*

READING: John 4:21-25; 14:15-26

KEY THOUGHT: When your Christian life becomes ordinary and habitual, you need the presence of the Holy Spirit to revive and use you.

I AM JESUS—*A Spirit-motivated Church*

"God revealed these things by his Spirit.
For his Spirit searches out everything and shows us God's deep secrets."

I COR. 2:10, *NLT*

I am Jesus who will send the Holy Spirit into your life and into your church. When you yield to the Holy Spirit and let Him control your life—and the life of your church—you will live and serve in a new experience of happiness and effectiveness. This book is about you being an exceptional follower of Me, so the first step is to ask the Holy Spirit to fill you (Eph. 5:18) and direct your daily life and service (Gal. 5:16, 25). Are you tired of striving for the things of outward satisfaction? Tired of trying to make a name for yourself and struggling to get ahead? Invite the Holy Spirit to control your life. Follow His lead and ask Him for power to do spiritual things you cannot do (Phil. 4:13).

Holy Spirit, come into my life to convict me of any ignorant sin (John 16:8).
Forgive me and cleanse all sin (1 John 1:9). Fill me with Your presence and lead
me today. Amen.

When the Holy Spirit comes into your life, He not only will show you where you have gone wrong, He will show you the Father's plan for your life: "I know the plans I have for you . . . they are plans for good and not for disaster, to give you a future and a hope" (Jer. 29:11, *NLT*). Why don't you pray for the Father's plans right now; they may have been a secret to you, but the Holy Spirit will reveal them to you.

Holy Spirit, I fall into a routine of earning money and taking care of business.
I yield to You. Come reveal Your plans for my life. I am excited about
my future. Amen.

READING: 1 Corinthians 2:1-15

KEY THOUGHT: The Holy Spirit has a plan for your life. Take the initiative to find it and do it.

Day 12

I AM JESUS—*In Revival*

*"Then if my people who are called by my name will humble themselves
and pray and seek my face and turn from their wicked ways,
I will hear from heaven and will forgive their sins and restore their land."*

2 CHRONICLES. 7:14, *NLT*

My people will have revival when they follow the formula in today's verse. First, they must humble themselves by admitting their selfish and egotistical desires by yielding everything to Me. Next, they must pray just as the first church prayed for 10 days between My ascension to heaven and Pentecost. The third step for revival is to seek My face. Remember, revival is described as pouring out My presence on My people. When the Shekinah glory cloud fell on the tabernacle, the people were revived. The fourth step is turning from your wicked ways. Quit all those activities that I disapprove of and repent of all known sin. That formula worked in the Old Testament and has worked in the church for 2,000 years. Are you ready for My presence to revive you and your church?

Lord, I admit I am selfish and seek my pride rather than Your glory. I cannot revive myself; I am too sinful. Send the Holy Spirit to revive me by visiting me daily and using me in service. Come, Holy Spirit, fill and revive me. Amen.

Your heart is the secret of revival. The Holy Spirit is always ready to come fill My church and energize My people. The heavenly Father seeks worship (John 4:27, 28), and I want to be preeminent in your life and church (Col. 1:18). We want you to be revived; it is the way you will live in heaven; it will be an added blessing and happiness to your life on Earth. Make a decision to start now to seek the Holy Spirit's presence in revival.

Lord, I simply ask You to revive me. I will obey You, follow You, and serve You. Fill me and use me. Amen.

READING: Colossian 1:15-20; Joel 2:12-32

KEY THOUGHT: The key to revival is found in 2 Chronicles 7:14, and you can determine the period when the Holy Spirit will come.

I AM JESUS—*Keeping Revival*

"So I say let the Holy Spirit guide your lives."
COLOSSIANS 5:16, *NLT*

"Since we are living by the Spirit, let us follow the Spirit's leading in every part of our lives."
GALATIANS 5:25, *NLT*

What happens when revival comes? You cannot just sit back to enjoy His presence. You must do something to keep revival going. When the Holy Spirit manifests His presence, keep living daily and do those things that brought revival. Follow His leading, go where He leads you, and do what He tells you to do. You have the Holy Spirit; now let Him work through you to testify to lost people and other believers who need revival. Do the work of ministry and let the Holy Spirit work through you. If you don't work with the Holy Spirit and allow Him to work through you, you will lose revival. The Spirit comes to work mightily in your church. If you cannot do what He has come to do, you will block out revival.

Holy Spirit, I want revival and ask You to pour Your presence on me and my church. I will let You lead me when You come, and I will minister with You. Send revival to my soul; I need it. Amen.

To keep revival in your life and church, you must continue doing those spiritual disciplines that brought revival in the first place. Don't grieve the Holy Spirit (Eph. 4:30), which is doing sinful things in your life. Also, don't quench the Holy Spirit (1 Thess. 5:19). When you snuff out a light, you quench its illumination. So don't do anything that is contrary to the holy nature of the Spirit. Don't snuff out His light.

Holy Spirit, come revive me and my church. I will not do anything to grieve You, nor will I put out the light of Your testimony in my life. I will pray as hard to keep revival as I did to originally get it. Amen.

READING: Acts 5:1-11; Eph. 4:20-32

KEY THOUGHT: When the Holy Spirit comes in revival, let Him guide you in your actions and life.

I AM JESUS— *Reviving Ministry*

"There are different kinds of spiritual gifts, but the same Spirit is the source of them all. There are different kinds of service . . . same Lord. God works in different ways, but it is the same God who does the work in all of us."

1 CORINTHIANS. 12:4-6, *NLT*

When the Holy Spirit is poured out on you in revival, it is not just for enjoyment. The Spirit comes into the church to enhance the ministry of each person in the church. He gives different spiritual gifts (abilities) to each believer. But He is the same Spirit working in each person but ministering differently. That is the beauty of one body: all the members work together for the same goal of carrying out the Great Commission. So to keep revival going, keep doing what you did to get revival. But remember, the Holy Spirit revives His church to carry out ministry for the Father. What are you and your church doing to keep revival fires burning?

Holy Spirit, You have given me spiritual gifts. I will use them to glorify the Father. I will work in harmony with You to keep revival going. Thank You for opportunities, and thank You for challenges. I will not give up. Amen.

Find the proper spiritual gift for you to use in ministry. First look in the rear-view mirror where you have been successful (Josh. 1:8), that might suggest where you should minister in the future. Listen to your friends and fellow workers; sometimes their counsel will help you know where to minister best (Prov. 10:14). Also, pray for the Holy Spirit to guide you into the most effective ministry for your spiritual gift. Finally, remember the principle of open doors. Opportunities may be the most effective place for your ministry.

Holy Spirit, I yield to You. Fill me for ministry. Guide me to ministry. Then use me in ministry. Amen.

READING: 1 Corinthians 12:1-31

KEY THOUGHT: When revival comes, the Holy Spirit is opening new doors of ministry. Find the best opportunity for your ministry and do it.

WEEK THREE

I AM JESUS
A Church Witnessing

Last week you read about the power of the Holy Spirit when He is poured out on a church. This week you will focus on using His power to witness to the world. You must first witness to them your salvation from sin and your transformation by the power of Jesus Christ. Then you must go in the power of the Holy Spirit to share the message with family, friends and the neighborhood. Finally, you will read how your church can plant churches around the world.

I AM JESUS—*A Witnessing Church*

"We cannot stop telling about everything we have seen and heard."
ACTS 4:20, *NLT*

I am Jesus, challenging you to witness to everyone about your salvation and love for Me. When I was on Earth, it was natural for Me to share My life and mission with everyone I touched. Now I live in you, so I want to speak through you to all you meet. Tell them of forgiveness of your sins and that I have a special place for your life (Jer. 2:9-11). But more than that, you are part of a New Testament church. I challenged My disciples to be My witnesses beginning at their house in Jerusalem and extending to Judea, which was the surrounding area. So you should join with your church to be My witnesses in your home area and outlying communities.

Lord, forgive me when I have been bashful and afraid to witness for You to my friends and family. Give me courage to share my testimony with others and give me wisdom to do it effectively. Amen.

I am Jesus, the power behind your testimony. I am the One who forgave all your sins when you called on Me for salvation. Now, I am the One living in your heart (Gal. 2:2). Let My presence in your life strengthen you to speak. Remember, those first disciples said, "We cannot stop telling about everything we have seen and heard" (Acts 4:20, *NLT*). Just share the Good News that changed your life, and it will change the lives of others.

Lord, thank You for the privilege of being a witness for You. I don't deserve this privilege, and I am not that good of a testimony, but I will tell my friends and fellow workers what You have done for me. Use me. Amen.

READING: Acts 1:1-9; 4:1-20

KEY THOUGHT: A witness is one who testifies to others what Jesus has done for them and how He has changed their life.

I AM JESUS—*A Church Growing*

"For we are both God's workers. And you are God's field."
1 CORINTHIANS. 3:9, *NLT*

*"Yes, I am the vine; you are the branches. Those who remain in me,
and I in them, will produce much fruit. For apart from me you can do nothing."*
JOHN 15:5, *NLT*

I am Jesus the Church. In Scripture My church is pictured as a garden, or a planted field, or a farm. It is a place where living seeds are planted to grow into food to eat or flowers for beauty. I produce eternal life when the seed of Scripture is planted in human hearts. In your church you see various believers in different stages of growth. Some are like newly planted seeds with growth potential. Some believers have new fruit; others have ripened fruit. But then others need pruning to get rid of dead branches that will kill, or fungus that will stunt growth: "I am the vine; you are the branches. Those who remain in me, and I in them, will produce much fruit" (John 15:5, *NLT*).

Lord, I want to be a healthy growing plant in Your garden. I need the water of the Word of God to grow, and the sunshine of answered prayer. I need cultivation around the roots to get life-giving air into my system. Lord, prune me where I need it. Amen.

I am the Church where you grow and bear fruit. I have life-giving energy to produce life through you. The secret to fruitfulness is your relationship with Me. Let My life flow into you to receive all the nutrients you need. I want to flow into you and through you. Growing a garden never ends; even after harvest in the fall, the field must be prepared for the next crop, next year. Your life is a garden that is life-growing.

Lord, it's a privilege to grow in Your garden. Produce life through me that is beautiful and nutritious. I want to accomplish everything in life that You have chosen for me to be and do. Amen.

READING: John 15:1-7

KEY THOUGHT: The church is pictured as a farm, or field, or garden that is planted, cultivated, and harvested to feed others.

I AM JESUS—*A Church Sharing the Good News*

"'We gave you strict orders never again to teach in this man's name!' he said.
'Instead, you have filled all Jerusalem with your teaching about him.'"

ACTS 5:28, *NLT*

The disciples went all over Jerusalem telling everyone about Me, Jesus. Their bold testimony got them in trouble with the authorities. They told their accusers, "We must obey God rather than any human authority" (v. 29). That is what I want you to do: tell everyone the Good News that I died to forgive their sins. Give them a testimony of My power that has changed your life. After all, I am more important to you than anything else (Phil. 1:21), and I can do more for them than anyone else. I need you to tell them the Good News. I can't do it; I am in heaven. Let Me minister to your friends and family through your testimony and acts of kindness. After all, you may be the only gospel testimony they ever experience.

Lord, I sometimes forget to share salvation with them. Forgive me. Fill me with
the power that You promised (Acts 1:8), and I will tell them that my sins are
forgiven, that I have been redeemed, and that I serve You. Amen.

The disciples filled Jerusalem teaching everyone about Me. They used every opportunity to share the gospel with everyone who would listen to them, and they did it at every available occasion and time. Now you should think of creative ways to tell friends and family about Me. The more often they hear about Me, the more likely they will be converted.

Lord, show me creative ways to share my testimony with friends and family.
Help me use every opportunity to give my testimony of how I got saved. Help me
to reach every friend and relative with the gospel. Help me use time wisely when I
am with them to share the power of Your saving grace in my life. Amen.

READING: Acts 5:17-42

KEY THOUGHT: The early church didn't limit their ministry to announced church times but used every available occasion and every available method to reach every available person with the gospel.

I AM JESUS—*A Church Reaching Lost People*

*"How I kept back nothing that was helpful, but proclaimed it to you,
and taught you publicly and from house to house, testifying to Jews, and also to Greeks,
repentance toward God and faith toward our Lord Jesus Christ."*

ACTS 20:20-22, *NKJV*

Paul shared the gospel in public gatherings and went house to house to try to win people to salvation. He was doing more than distributing Christian literature or inviting people to attend church. He was sharing the gospel by "testifying to Jews, and also to Greeks, repentance toward God and faith toward our Lord Jesus Christ" (v. 21). Paul did what some modern-day churches forget—he evangelized. I am Jesus who gave the Great Commission to My followers to preach "into all the world . . . to every creature" (Mark 16:15, *NKJV*). In Matthew 28:19 (*NKJV*), I also said, "Make disciples of all the nations (tribes)." Therefore, evangelize every person, in every part of the world, and disciple new believers of all people groups. Is your church obeying Me?

*Lord, forgive me when I had a hard heart or was unresponsive to Your
Commission. Burden my heart to pray for lost people and may I attempt to reach
them with the gospel. May I win at least one person to salvation. Amen.*

I am Jesus who commanded you to evangelize all. You could do it several ways. You could do personal evangelism, i.e., one on one. Or you could get involved in your church's evangelistic outreach. Then there are other para-church organizations that are reaching lost people. You could minister with them in other ways to fully support foreign missions with your time, talent and offerings. If today believers were as evangelistic as the first-century church in evangelism, the Great Commission could be finished.

*Lord, I pray for churches everywhere to work hard to fulfill the
Great Commission. Forgive our failures and give us spiritual power to
reach them all. Amen.*

READING: Acts 20:13-38

KEY THOUGHT: When Jesus gave the Great Commission, He expected His followers to be both enthusiastic and energetic in spreading it to all people.

I AM JESUS—*A Body Exercising*

*"Their responsibility is to equip God's people to do his work a
nd build up the church, the body of Christ."*

EPHESIANS 4:12, *NLT*

I am Jesus, the Church body. Did you see today's verse that said, "Build up the church"? How do you build up a body? Exercise! Not once but by doing it many times. To build up My Church body, you need to win souls. Not once but many times. But exercise cannot be a little effort, not to build a physical body. You must exercise till you sweat, till you are exhausted. Have you tried to win lost people with all your heart and energy? Have you continued trying to win souls till you were exhausted? The gym instructor tells you; "no pain, no gain." So I challenge you "no total effor, no church growth." One more thing about exercise: it gets harder each day, more intense each day, more difficult each day. Have you gotten to the place where it is difficult to win people to Me? If so, then you are just beginning. Keep up the hard work, the smart work, the rewarding work.

Lord, I want my church body to grow. Sometimes time I see no growth; at other times I see little growth. But I will not stop. I will keep exercising till I see measurable growth, consistent growth. Amen.

I am Jesus, your Church body. Don't think of Me as an organization, or budget, or program. I am working on you to build up My church. I am the Church body reaching out to capture lost people to incorporate them into My body. I cannot do it without you, and you cannot do it without Me. We are church! Let's get lost people into our body.

Lord, when I am not effective, show me how to serve You. When I have little fruit, make me more effective. When I am discouraged, speak to me, motivate me, fill me. Then send me out to serve You. Amen.

READING: Ephesians 4:1-16

KEY THOUGHT: Just as a physical body is built with exercise, so too the spiritual church body is built by spiritual exercise.

Day 20

I AM JESUS—*Adding to My Church*

*"Those who believed what Peter said were baptized and added to the church that day—
about 3,000 in all. All the believers devoted themselves to the apostles' teaching,
and to fellowship, and to sharing in meals (including the Lord's Supper), and to prayer."*

ACTS 2:41-42, *NLT*

I am Jesus, the Church body of Christ left on the earth when I was resurrected to ascend to heaven. There were 120 praying in the Upper Room (Acts 1:15). After Peter preached a powerful sermon on Pentecost, "Those who believed . . . were baptized and added to the church" (Acts 1:41, *NLT*). A few weeks later Peter preached again: "The number of believers now totaled about 5,000" (Acts 4:4, *NLT*). These were the heads of families, so about 20,000 were in the church. Next, "believers rapidly multiplied" (Acts 6:1, *NLT*). Then believers grew exponentially: "Believers greatly increased" (Acts 6:7, NLT). Finally, it was no longer the growth of believers, "The churches . . . were multiplied" (Acts 9:31, *NKJV*). When the number of churches grew exponentially, that explosion was super-aggressive growth. Pray for that increase in your church.

> *Lord, thank You for my salvation and for those who have found salvation in
> my church. I want to see exponential growth in my church: "Increase our faith"
> (Luke 17:5, NKJV). You are the God who caused the first church to grow;
> do it again. Amen.*

But the church in Jerusalem had more than numbers. It was growing internally and spiritually. They were learning the Word daily (Acts 1:42, 5:42). They continued praying (Acts 1:42, 5:31), they gave sacrificially (Acts 1:44, 11:29), and God gave them exponential blessings (Acts 1:42-47). Because they followed Me fully, they became exceptional Christians who built an exponential church. If you and all the others in your church grew mightily, so would your church.

> *Lord, I pray to be an exceptional believer so that my church will grow
> exponentially. Amen.*

READING: Acts 2:1-13, 42-47; 4:1-4

KEY THOUGHT: The early church had exponential growth because the believers were exceptional followers of Jesus.

Day 21

I AM JESUS—*Continuous Witnessing*

"The high priest confronted them (the church) . . .
you have filled all Jerusalem with your teaching."

ACTS 5:28, *NLT*

"And every day, in the temple and from house to house,
they continued to preach and teach . . . Jesus is Messiah."

ACTS 5:42, *NLT*

I am a church that continually witnesses the message of salvation. I tell every person from young to old, from rich to poor, and from Jew to Gentile. But more than that, I want to witness all the time in every place. Why do My followers witness continuously? Because I said, "I am the way . . . no one can come to the Father except through Me" (John 14:6, *NLT*). I am the only One who can save all people. And I love all people (John 3:16). So witness to them My love. Not only that, invite them into My body—the church—the greatest privilege in the world, with the greatest benefits and blessings. Since you are My followers, you must witness about Me to all.

Lord, thank You for saving me and transforming me with the gospel
message. Forgive me for not witnessing to others. Give me an inner
compulsion to witness to my lost friends and family. Amen.

My command is one more reason to witness to all people, at all times, using all methods: "You shall be witnesses to Me" (Acts 1:8, *NKJV*). When you become a Christian, the Holy Spirit comes into your life. Now let Him use you to witness about Me in your home area to win your Jerusalem. Then witness in the surrounding areas, next the "large" state or provinces, and finally use all your witnessing influence to change the world.

Lord, I will obey and begin witnessing to family and friends today. Amen.

READING: Acts 5:29-42; 11:19-21

KEY THOUGHT: It is imperative for every follower to witness to everyone they know to reach and change the world.

WEEK FOUR

I AM JESUS:
A Teaching Church

When you evangelize new converts that come to salvation, then you must obey the second part of the Great Commission, i.e., "Teaching them to obey all things I taught you" (Matt. 28:20, ELT). Super-aggressive evangelism must lead to exponential teaching. The new converts must be taught about Me and what I can do for them. Teaching begins at the earliest age and extends to the senior citizen members. The ministry of teaching includes the new converts receiving salvation and extends to the more mature believers in the church. It includes teaching Bible content, Christian living, attitudes, and all other matter. What happens when a church obeys the teaching mandate? "I am with you to the ends of the earth" (Matt. 28:20, ELT).

Day 22

I AM JESUS—*Exponential Teaching*

"Daily in the temple and house to house, they ceased not to teach and preach."

ACTS 5:42, *KJV*

"The church leaders said, 'We will give ourselves continually to prayer and to the ministry of the Word.'"

ACTS 6:4, *KJV*

I am the early church that continually gave itself to the Word of God. The leaders gave themselves to teaching, and new converts gave themselves to learning. The new church was grounded on Scripture and teaching. As a result, individuals followed Me. And that is why the Christian experienced exponential growth. My Word is alive (John 6:63), and it is powerful (Heb. 4:12). When you properly teach the Word of God, you are preparing for explosive growth. Why? Because super-aggressive teaching of Scripture leads to exponential growth

Lord, I want my church to experience exponential growth. I will learn the Word of God for myself, and I will teach it super-aggressively. Then, Lord, I ask You to grow the church and change the world. Amen.

I am Jesus, who will bless the church with exponential growth when the foundation is laid with solid Bible teaching. Then you must follow with aggressive faith, aggressive witnessing, and aggressive outreach of the gospel. Do you want to change the world? There is a predetermined formula that works.

Lord, I pray for my church to change the world. But first, Lord, change me. Make me a super-aggressive witness. Then, Lord, help me motivate people in my church to a greater vision. Then, Lord, help us change our world. Then perhaps we can change the rest of the world. Amen.

READING: Acts 2:42-46; 4:4-24; 8:4-8

KEY THOUGHT: The gospel is the only message that saves people from hell, and the Great Commission is the only method to preach the gospel to everyone to change the world.

Day 23

I AM JESUS—*Teaching New Followers*

"Teach these new disciples to obey all the commands I have given you."
MATTHEW 28:20, *NLT*

"Those . . . added to the church . . . devoted themselves to the apostle's teaching."
ACTS 2:41-42, *NLT*

I am Jesus, teaching new believers. Did you see two things in today's verses? First, I commanded the church to teach new disciples all My commands. Second, the church got people saved and then they taught them. Early exponential church growth was based on teaching new converts My commands. Is your church doing that today? When hundreds in a neighborhood become new followers, teach them what to believe and train them how to live for Me. Do that and you will change a neighborhood. How can you change the world? Get people saved, then teach them what to believe and how to live for Me. Then reproduce that result in another new church.

> *Lord, forgive me for not studying Your Word more and knowing You better. Help me learn great truths about You I don't know. Send the Holy Spirit to teach me (John 14:16) and help me remember (John 14:26). Help me to be a learning, growing, useful follower of Yours. Amen.*

I am the Church, and in Me all types of teaching go on. Babies are being taught; older people are being taught. People are being taught how to serve, how to lead, and how to be better parents and examples to lost people. All kinds of people are teaching: church leaders, older women teaching younger women, parents teaching their children. And teaching is going on in Sunday school classes, for all ages, and all needs, and all different subjects. I want My church to be a teaching church.

> *Lord, thank You for my parents, who taught me many things. I will teach my family and children. Thank You for all types of teachers in my church. Help me learn, grow, and serve You better. I will teach. Amen.*

READING: Matthew 13:1-23

KEY THOUGHT: Scripture is filled with commands and illustrations of teaching. You can't build a church on teaching; you build it on evangelism. You can't build a church without teaching.

I AM JESUS—A Teaching Church

"But the comforter, the Holy Spirit . . . He will teach you all things."
JOHN 14:26, *NLT*

"When He, the Spirit of truth, is come, He will guide you into all truth."
JOHN 16:13, *NLT*

The One who guides your understanding in My church is the Holy Spirit. Did you see one of His names is *Spirit of Truth?* He will guide you into truth. Guiding is what a teacher does: "Teaching is the guidance of learning activities." Teaching is not just telling a lesson. No! A teacher guides the learning activities; it is learning that changes the life of the student. The teacher hasn't taught until the student has learned the intended lesson. It is the Holy Spirit in the heart of the teacher Who guides the learning process.

Lord, thank You for all I have learned. I don't know all. I want to learn even more of Your Word and more about You. I want to teach others what I am learning; give me a classroom of one or many. Use me to teach. Amen.

When Philip witnessed to the Ethiopian eunuch in his chariot, he asked, "Do you understand what you read?" He was reading the book of Isaiah. The Ethiopian official answered, "How can I, unless someone instructs me?" (Acts 8:31, *NKJV*). Did you see that word *guide?* Both the Holy Spirit and human teachers are needed to guide people to understand the Word of God.

Holy Spirit, I cannot teach, but You can do it through me. I cannot change the life of another; but Holy Spirit, You can do it through me. Come, Holy Spirit, fill my life. Use my teaching. I want to change the life of another to be like Jesus. Amen.

READING: John 14:16-26; Acts 8:26-39

KEY THOUGHT: Great teachers guide the learning experience of students, but the Holy Spirit must guide both teacher and student.

I AM JESUS—*Prepare and Teach*

"Study to shew thyself approved unto God, a workman that needeth not to be ashamed, rightly dividing the word of truth."
2 TIMOTHY 2:15, *NLT*

"Continue in the things you have learned."
2 TIMOTHY 3:14, *NLT*

"Meditate on these things."
1 TIMOTHY 4:15, *NLT*

I am a church with human teachers and learners. Before you can teach, you must learn the lessons you would teach. The church is primarily a place of evangelism, and second, a place of education. Those who know the most Christian doctrine should teach the most. Those who know best how to live for Christ teach best. And those who know Christ intimately teach and change lives of others. What do you know most and best about your Christian faith? How much of it have you taught? Those who know best teach others who have learned.

Lord, forgive me for being lazy and not learning more about my faith and knowing You better. Teach me those things I don't know. Show me where I am ignorant, so I can learn and grow and have intimate fellowship with You (Phil. 3:10-14). Amen.

I am a church on a teaching mission. You will never know it all, and you will never know enough. You were born in this world with a blank slate mind. How much you learn will determine how much you will grow. And how practically you learn the Christian life will determine how effective you will live for Me.

Lord, I will read Your Word, repeatedly. I will study Your Word, dividing truth into small sections to learn. I will memorize Your Word, hiding it in my heart (Ps. 119:11). Then I will meditate on Your Word, so its life principles control my life (Josh. 1:8; Ps. 1:5). Amen.

READING: Joshua 1:6-9; Psalms 1:1-6; 119:9-16

KEY THOUGHT: My church shall be a place of teaching-learning, because neither are effective until both are operative.

I AM JESUS—*A Reproducing Church*

"You have heard me teach things that have been confirmed by many reliable witnesses.
Now teach these truths to other trustworthy people who will be able to pass them on to others."

2 TIMOTHY. 2:2, *NLT*

I am a church that will die if the children and new converts are not taught church belief and the practices I taught you. In today's scripture, Paul taught young Timothy the principle of reproduction. Paul was the first generation passing Christianity on to the second generation. But it doesn't stop there. Timothy must then teach everything he learned to the third generation, called "trustworthy people." This means they were worthy of the trust Timothy had in them. Then the third generation must teach the fourth generation. They are called "others." What Paul taught was not properly learned until it influenced the third generation. How do we know Timothy did as good a job as Paul? Because the third generation passed the lesson on to the fourth generation. Is your church teaching its children, grandchildren, and great-grandchildren?

Lord, I have failed in many ways. But I don't want to fail as a teacher. Help me
teach Your doctrine and the Christian life to my children then my grandchildren
and ultimately my great-grandchildren. Amen.

Let's see how this works. I taught Andrew in his first day of ministry (John 1:38-40). Then Andrew brought his brother Peter (second generation) to be a follower of Mine (John 1:41-42). Then Peter preached on Pentecost and over 300 got saved. They could be described as the third spiritual generation. Then, they went back to their homes and spread the gospel, i.e., a fourth generation of Jesus followers.

Lord, I want fruit in my life. May I help someone to salvation. Then may I teach
them what to believe and how to live, so they can go to teach someone else.
Lord, multiply my life. Amen.

READING: John 1:35-42; Acts 2:5-12, 41-47

KEY THOUGHT: The secret to successful teaching is when your students can share what they have learned with someone else and then they pass it on.

Day 27

I AM JESUS—*A Teaching Church for the Young*

"And you must commit yourselves wholeheartedly to these commands . . . repeat them again and again to your children . . . when you are at home . . . on the road . . . going to bed and . . . getting up."
DEUTERONOMY 6:6-7, *NLT*

"Timothy . . . your genuine faith . . . first filled your grandmother Lois, and your mother Eunice."
2 TIMOTHY 1:5, *NLT*

I want My church diligently teaching all children. Timothy was an early church leader who was first taught by his grandmother, then his mother. Paul reminded him, "You have been taught the holy scriptures from childhood" (2 Tim. 3:15, *NLT*). That is the example for all churches today. When this standard is reached, then growing exponential churches can change the world by producing reproducing believers. Satan wants to capture everyone in My church, and he will start with those most vulnerable—the children. Protect your children; teach them about Me. Guarantee your church's future; teach the children.

Lord, forgive me where I have been slack teaching children. They are so young and have great futures before them. Help me reach children with salvation, and then teach them the Scriptures. I want a strong leader like Timothy to come out of my church. So I will pray and teach. Amen.

A child is born with a blank slate. They must learn to talk, walk and feed themselves. They must be taught to read, write and communicate. Make sure they learn basic Christianity, how to follow Me. Then they must learn basic beliefs, knowledge about God, sin, salvation and Christian service. The more they learn, the stronger Christians they will become. The better they are trained, the more they can do for Me and the church. I love churches that teach the young.

Lord, it's clear You have commanded us to teach the children. Forgive me and forgive my church where we have failed. I want to teach children and I want my children to be strong future leaders for You. Amen.

READING: Deuteronomy 6:1-9; Mark 10:13-16; Acts 16:1-5

KEY THOUGHT: Everything you know about Christianity will be lost to the church when you die, so teach the young so that they can replace you and they can teach the next generation.

Day 28

I AM JESUS—*Teaching Scriptures*

"But you must remain faithful to the things you have been taught . . . the holy Scriptures from childhood, and they have given you the wisdom to receive the salvation . . . all Scripture is inspired by God and is useful to teach us what is true and to make us realize what is wrong in our lives."

2 TIMOTHY 3:14-16, *NLT*

The church teaches Scriptures not just to know it or be smart but to lead you to salvation. Timothy was saved because the Bible had been taught to him as a child. The Bible is the most important lesson for a child to learn in church. The Bible will convict you of wrong doing (2 Tim. 3:16), so you will get saved. The Bible has My life in it (John 6:63); it will give you eternal life. The Bible will help you find a plan and purpose for your life. The Bible will give you assurances of salvation (1 John 5:13) and take away doubt and fear. The Bible will help you find My presence in prayer. Don't you need to ask Me something (John 15:7)?

Lord, I will study Your Scriptures for confidence and direction. Guide me with Your Word (Ps. 119:105). I want to hide Your Word in my heart to keep from sinning against You (Ps. 119:11). Amen.

I am the Word of God incarnate (John 1:1, 14). I teach My Word in My church to transform sinners into children of God and to make babes in Christ grow to maturity (Heb. 5:11-14). I teach My Word that grows work-men into powerful pulpit preachers. My Word will make silly girls into godly women intercessors. Let's teach My Word.

Lord, help me take every opportunity to teach Your Word. Help me to teach all people—new believers and wise people—Your Word. I love Your Word; it has changed my life. Use me to teach others to also change them. Amen.

READING: 2 Timothy 3:10-17; John 1:1-18

KEY THOUGHT: Teach the Bible to produce many different changes in people, in many different types of people.

WEEK FIVE

I AM JESUS
A Ministering and Serving Church

This fifth week focuses on the ways you can minister in your church. Everyone has a spiritual gift or ability to serve the Father. That ability gives them an obligation to minister with all their heart for the glory of the Father. Also, it will lead to the exponential expansion of the church. The secret of a growing church is when all members minister and serve sacrificially to carry out the Great Commission. When that is done, the church will continue growing exponentially to bring glory to God the Father.

I AM JESUS—*A Church Ministering*

"A great famine . . . so the believers in Antioch decided to send relief . . .
everyone giving as much as they could."
ACTS 11:28-29, *NLT*

When a church is ministering to the poor, needy and helpless, that is Me showing My love through My church. It may be the hands of men and women in the church, but it is My hands. My church should never allow people to starve; it should give to demonstrate My love. Then they will listen to the gospel that will save them. You must think both physical and spiritual needs. You cannot minister one without the other. Look at My example while on Earth. I ministered to people whether or not they were My followers. And many began following Me because of "love in action."

Lord, I confess to being stingy sometimes. Forgive me. Help me look at people
through Your eyes. Help me look beyond a physical problem into their heart.
Then help me to communicate Your gospel to people. Healing the physical body is
love in action, but healing a lost soul is eternal. Amen.

No church can do all things to help all people at all times. But begin at home; minister to those in your family then those in your neighborhood. But remember, it is not giving money, or food, or physical healing. It is about your relationship to Me. Let My compassion flow through you. Then it is about your relationship to your family and church. You cannot neglect them. Then look beyond your church limits; look for avenues to help, heal, and offer eternal salvation.

Lord, I want to minister for You. Show me how, where, and when.
Here am I, use me. Amen.

READING: Acts 11:19-30; 6:1-7

KEY THOUGHT: All humans ought to be compassionate and helpful to those around them, but the followers of Jesus must give first, give most, and give the gospel.

I AM JESUS—*A Church of Ministers*

"Determined to send relief . . . by the hands of Barnabas and Saul."
ACTS 11:29-30, *NLT*

"But the word of God grew and multiplied . . . they returned . . .
when they had fulfilled their ministry."
ACTS 12:24-25, *NLT*

My church prospers when ministry is properly done. In today's verses, the church at Antioch sent money and supplies to Jerusalem because of a famine. But the money didn't just feed hungry people. There was spiritual ministry with their money: "The word of God grew and multiplied" (Acts 12:24, *NKJV*). That means two things. First, the influence of Scripture spread over the area. Next, people responded to the God of the Bible by preaching of those who fed them; some were saved, and the church grew. Second, it meant the church was growing in understanding and use of the Word.

Lord, thank You for the opportunity of ministering both to the physical and
spiritual needs of others. I will not do one without the other; I will do both at the
same time. Give me a heart for needy people, both physical and spiritual. Amen.

In today's passage, Barnabas and Saul left Antioch to travel a long distance to minister to the physical needs of Jerusalem. That is the city that crucified Me and persecuted My church. Why go there? Remember I said, "Repay no one evil for evil . . . if your enemy is hungry feed him" (Rom. 12:17, 20, *NLT*). Give help, give the Gospel, and give yourself to prayer for them. Remember, I forgave those who crucified Me: "Father forgive them" (Luke 23:34, *NKJV*). Learn to minister in many ways.

Lord, I want to give to others just as others gave to me. But I want to do more
to minister to others than they ministered to me. I want to minister as
You ministered. Amen.

READING: Luke 6:27-38; Romans 12:17-21

KEY THOUGHT: Minister to the physical needs of those who are not My followers, even those who persecute My followers.

I AM JESUS—*Exponential Ministry*

"You have filled all Jerusalem with your teaching about Him."
ACTS 5:28, *NLT*

"Publically from house to house."
ACTS 20:20, *NLT*

Did you see the pattern in the early church? They were saturating their city with My teaching. Exponential ministry is serving people at every available time, with every available means or methods, to reach everyone available. That means start early, minister all day, and finish late. It means using more than one area of service, going to more than just one group of people. This is a picture of revival because they served in the power of the Holy Spirit. Also, it is a picture of exponential ministry. When your church is unselfish, you are a testimony to Me and the way I do ministry.

Lord, move me out of my comfort zone. My selfishness keeps me from helping a lot of people. Lord give me "Jesus eyes" to see the millions as You see them. Give me "Jesus hands" to serve as You ministered. Amen.

When you are saturating your neighborhood with ministry, you are giving exponential ministry. Not only are you sacrificing your time and giving resources, you are identifying with Me. Remember, I serve sacrificially, which means My example will motivate you to ministry. One way to judge if your ministry is exponential, look at your hands: do you have anything left? Also, look at your feet: have you gone everywhere to minister? Look into your heart: do you have any compassion that you have withheld? Then I will say, "Well done good and faithful servant. I will have much reward for you in heaven" (Matt. 25:21, ELT).

Lord, use my hands to help the needy. Use my feet to take me to those who need help. Fill my heart with gratitude to You. Amen.

READING: Acts 20:16-37

KEY THOUGHT: Another word for exponential is *saturation*. It is giving all types of ministry and all your energy, all the time to do as much as you can do.

I AM JESUS—*Your Example in Ministry*

"People were brought out into the streets on beds and mats . . . crowds came from . . . around Jerusalem bringing their sick . . . all were healed."

ACTS 5:15-16, *NLT*

I am Jesus who serves others through your hands and your sacrificial service. There was exponential ministry because "More and more people believed and were brought to the Lord" (Acts 5:14, *NLT*). When you and your church give more than expected by the crowd, expect exponential results: "Believers were added to the Lord" (Acts 5:14). Isn't that what you desire and pray for and minister for? If your church doesn't have many lost people coming to get saved, then you and other church members must go out to where they are located. Do what? Give a "cup of water to drink in My name" (Mark 9:41, *NKJV*). The secret of exponential ministry is not what you can do, but what you can give. What will you give?

Lord, I bring My selfish heart to You. Heal it and transform it.
Give me Your heart for ministry and I will follow Your example of serving
in Your name. Amen.

Make your assembly a serving church to needs, no matter who and where and when. You cannot help everyone, but you can have a heart for all. You cannot do all types of service, but you can start with what you can do. If you—and all others in your church—begin serving other people, you will be amazed what multiple hands can do, and how much they can accomplish. And you will be amazed at the multiple times you are ministering.

Lord, the problem with humble service is not location or ability to serve.
The issue is my inner desire. I am selfish by nature. Forgive me and lead me
to a task I can do for You. Amen.

READING: Mark 9:33-41; Acts 5:1-16

KEY THOUGHT: Your example in ministry is Jesus who ministered in many ways, at many times, doing many types of humanitarian service.

I AM JESUS—*Serving People*

"But among you it will be different.
Whoever wants to be a leader among you must be your servant."
MARK 10:43, *NLT*

I came to serve people; follow My example. Serve other believers and serve those who are lost. Why? First, because the nature of love is giving, and I gave all for people. I serve because I love them, both My followers and those who do not follow Me. Ask the Father to give you a divine love. Second, serving is My nature. Notice how Paul described Me: "Though He was God . . . He gave up His divine privileges; He took the humble position of a slave" (Phil. 2:6-7, *NLT*). Ask the Father to give you a serving heart. But there is a third reason: because others are in need. The world is full of needy people. By ministering you open them up to salvation, and you actually alleviate their pain. They need you.

Lord, I want to minister to other people as You did. But serving is not always natural. I want my way and I want my needs satisfied, and I want it on my time Forgive me, cleanse me, and change me. Serve me so I can serve others. Amen.

At the Last Supper, "I got up . . . took off My robe . . . poured water into a basin . . . began to wash the disciple's feet" (John 13:4-5, *NLT*). Remember, they had just been arguing over who was the greatest. When I asked you to follow Me, I invited you, "Deny yourself, and take up your cross daily" (Luke 9:23, *ELT*). My example should motivate you to exponential serving. That is going beyond what a human could do; it's divine motivation.

Lord, I will follow Your example. I will serve others. Even when I don't want to, that is the time I will do it. Even when I think the task is too demeaning, I will do it just as You did. Amen.

READING: John 13:1-10

KEY THOUGHT: You must follow Jesus' example of serving when your example will help others, just as Jesus gave an example.

I AM JESUS—*A Whole Healthy Ministering Body*

"He makes the whole body fit together perfectly. As each part does its own special work, it helps the other parts grow, so that the whole body is healthy and growing and full of love."

EPHESIANS 4:16, *NLT*

I live in you and all other members of your local church so that My body is healthy, growing and possesses the divine attributes of love. Look at the phrase "helps the other parts grow." Have you ever thought that your growth in ministry will help others in your church grow? Sometimes you will have a direct ministry to them, such as teaching, counseling, or actually serving them. At other times you will work alongside them so they are motivated by your example. At other times, you may not touch their lives directly; they may not even know you; but as you make the body stronger, they benefit. When the water level is raised in a lake, all the boats on the lake go up. Ask God to make your ministry helpful to others.

Lord, I love to serve You in ministry; You are my primary motivation. But I also love my church and its people. Help me minister effectively to individuals and to the whole church. I want my spiritual gifts used, and I want Your body to grow. Amen.

You serve in ministry because you are motivated by your spiritual gifts (abilities). These gifts make you effective in ministry. But also My love will move you to action. Then there are many other motivations for serving Me. Remember, serving is not the main thing, nor are results the main motivation. It is your relationship with Me. You minister because "I am in you, and you are in Me" (John 14:20, ELT). When you strengthen your relationship with Me, your ministry will grow and be strengthened.

Lord, I serve others because of You.
Use my ministry to help others serve You better. Amen.

READING: Eph. 4:1-16; 1 Cor. 12:1-31

KEY THOUGHT: Jesus wants all in His body to serve as best as possible so they will grow peacefully and the body will grow completely.

Day 35

I AM JESUS— *Using Every Available Person*

"Then the church . . . became stronger as the believers . . .
with the encouragement of the Holy Spirit . . . grew in numbers."

ACTS 9:31, *NLT*

There are three principles in today's verse that should encourage you and all other followers of Me in your local church. First, all believers from all churches were encouraged in their ministry by the Holy Spirit. Not just the pastor and apostles, but "believers." So pray that you and all others in your church will have a fruitful ministry. Second, it took all—leaders and followers—to strengthen a church. If members in your church are not involved in ministry, then those weak links weaken the entire church. Third, new believers were saved and added to the church, and at the same time, new churches were being planted and the Great Commission was being fulfilled.

Lord, I don't want to be a weak link in the chain of ministry in my
church. Show me what to do and what more I can do in my present
ministry. Then use me in ministry and use my example to encourage
others in their ministry. Amen.

My goal for your church is to involve every member, each doing their ministry to serve every need at all places and all times. When that happens, your church will grow and each member will grow in Christ. Then exponential ministry will produce exponential growth.

Lord, I pray to grow to maturity as I serve in ministry for You.
I also pray that my church would grow to involve more in ministry
and may my church grow in strength and outreach. Amen.

READING: Acts 9:20-31; Eph. 4:1-16

KEY THOUGHT: Jesus wants everyone in the church to use their ministry, so each will grow to spiritual maturity and the whole body would also grow to complete the Great Commission.

WEEK SIX

I AM JESUS:
My Church Expectations

Your reading and prayers this week will focus on My expectations for My followers and My church. You will examine the powerful commands I give to My followers and what I expect them to do. Then you will examine My various ways the Great Commission will produce exponential growth. Just as the early church was aggressive in testifying its faith to the world, so too today your church can become an exponential body of believers; let's change the world. The secret is, when all members realize what they can do for Me, and they make a commitment to do it, they will see exceptional ministry. Together they will have exponential results.

Day 36

I AM JESUS—*A Church Reaching Average People*

"God in his wisdom saw . . . the world would never know him through human wisdom . . . few of you were wise in the world's eyes or powerful, or wealthy . . . rather God chose to use the (weak) . . . things counted as nothing . . . by the wise."

1 CORINTHIANS 1:21, 27-28, *NLT*

I am Jesus who calls average people and strengthens them to be above average—exceptional. I don't always call those with the highest IQ or the most money or powerful positions. I empower common people to do extraordinary ministry. When an average follower leads a millionaire to Christ, it's not to get his/her money, but to save him/her from hell. Average people do it because of My love through them, My power through their testimony, and the supernatural life in the Word of God that transforms the unsaved. If I can use Gideon who was the least important in his family to defeat over 100,000 Midianties, what can I do with you?

> *Lord, I am not big in the world's eyes, and I am not important in the eyes of business, but I want You to use me. Help me get someone saved and influence others. Use me in a way greater than my ability. Amen.*

I am Jesus who fills your life with My presence. Don't try to do it by yourself. Let Me work through you. Let My light shine through your words, and actions. Focus on Me—not yourself—and I can use you to change one person or one family. Do you think you could change a neighborhood? Or more?

> *Lord, all I have to offer You is my life, my mind, my love, and my desire to serve You. Come forgive my sin and overcome my weaknesses. Fill me with the Holy Spirit's power and give me opportunities to serve You. Amen.*

READING: Acts 6:1-6; 8:4-40

KEY THOUGHT: I use ordinary followers to do extraordinary things through their yieldedness and My power.

Day 37

I AM JESUS—*A Church of All Nationalities*

"Some . . . began preaching . . . only to Jews. However the church in Antioch . . . preached to the Gentiles . . . a large number of Gentiles believed."

ACTS 11:20-21, ELT

"It doesn't matter if you are a Jew, or a Gentile . . . barbaric, uncivilized, slave, or free. Christ . . . lives in all of us."

COLOSSIANS 3:11, *NLT*

I am a church made up of men, women, children and all cultures of the world. The children sing a chorus in Sunday school, "Red and yellow, black or white, they are precious in His sight." That is the essence of My New Testament church. Because everyone is in Me, they are in My church. I live in people of every ethnic race, and through them I reach their family, friends, and neighbors. Have I reached you and your family? If so, I want to work through you to evangelize all your relationships. You may be the only one who can lead them to salvation. If you don't do it, who else can I use?

Lord, thank You for my salvation, and thank You for those who brought the Gospel to my family. I pray for everyone in my family to become a Christian— young and old—men and women—all of them. Use me to reach people with the Gospel that no one else could do. Amen.

I am a church made up of all cultures of the world. When you get to heaven I invite you to join in the choir to sing hallelujah and praise to the Father. What culture are you from? You will join all people from every tribe (ethnic group) and language, all with a color different from yours and a language different from you—will you be comfortable in My heaven?

Lord, I love Your church of many colors and many language, and many cultures. I pray for the Gospel to reach every tribe in the world. Help me to do my part to carry the Gospel to the ends of the earth. Amen.

READING: Gal. 3:26-27; Rev. 5:8-10

KEY THOUGHT: I commanded the Gospel to be preached to every tribe (ethnic group) until all groups have heard the Gospel.

I AM JESUS—*A Church of the Rich and Poor*

"Joseph . . . nicknamed Barnabas . . . from the tribe of Levi . . . came from the island of Cyprus. He sold a field he owned and brought the money to the apostles."

ACTS 5:36-37, *NLT*

I am a church made up of all kinds of people—rich and poor—from all different places. One of the first missionaries was Barnabas, who owned a field but sold it and gave all the money to Me. He remembered what I told the rich young ruler: "One thing you haven't done. sell all your possessions and give the money to the poor" (Luke 18:22, *NLT*). Barnabas did that, and the apostles used that money to give to the poor. When a person sacrifices everything to Me, I can use them, like I did Barnabas. It is not wrong to possess money; it is wrong for money to possess you. Remember the man who had five bags of silver (Matt. 25:16). When he used his money properly for My purpose, I commanded him and gave him five more bags. The one who had only one bag of silver selfishly hoarded it and hid it. I took it away from him (Matt. 25:24-25). It's not wrong to have money and use it for My ministry. It is wrong when money has you.

Lord, forgive me for being selfish and stingy. I yield everything to You. Take control of all My money, possessions and "stuff." Use them for Your glory. Amen.

I am a church made up of rich and poor. Remember the widow woman giving her money in the temple. She didn't give a lot, "two small coins." Then I said, "She has given more . . . she has given everything she has" (Luke 21:2, 4, *NLT*). It is not what you give to Me; it is your attitude of humility. It is not how much you give; it is how much you hang on to after you give to Me.

Lord, You own everything—the earth, the cattle in the fields and the gold in the mines. I give You everything. Use it for Your purpose. Whatever You leave for me to use, I will spend it for Your glory. Amen.

READING: Luke 21:1-4; Matt. 25:14-30

KEY THOUGHT: There are different levels of income among My people in My church. They should surrender all to My use and use wisely what is left over for them.

I AM JESUS—*A Unified Church Working*

"We will speak . . . growing in every way more and more like Christ,
who is the head of his body, the church."

EPHESIANS 4:15, *NLT*

I am Jesus, a unified body. When you plant Me in a neighborhood, lost people will be converted to become members of My body. Then each believer will grow in spiritual maturity, and as all grow together to be an effective body, they will minister in that neighborhood for Me. Like a physical body, they will work in coordinated unity. But each believer will have different spiritual gifts, different personalities, and different backgrounds. Each will bring different abilities to make My body effective. Again like a physical body, each member of the church body will work in mutual fellowship. Just as each member of a body gives different life to the whole body, so too each believer will contribute richness and variety to ministry. Then there is dependency, the little finger needs the arm to reach out, and they both need eyes to guide what they do. A small member like an ear needs a large member like a backbone.

Lord, everyone in my church is not like me, and they don't function like me and
they don't have my priorities. Give me love for the uniqueness of each and for
the strength of each. I will not criticize another; help me to see the good points in
others that You see. Amen.

I am Jesus, the head of the body. I made everyone different in your church, but they all belong to Me and depend on Me just as you do. Keep your eyes on Me, your Lord. Keep giving 100 percent of your talents to carry out the Great Commission. Pray for others with different personalities, support others with different talents, and work with all to make this body healthy. Then all believers will worship the Father, bringing others to salvation, and helping build the spirituality of all.

Lord forgive me when I think only of my personal needs. Help me support
my whole church body, love all members, and build up the weak and needy.
Use my church as a body to complete the Great Commission. Amen.

READING: 1 Cor. 12:1-31

KEY THOUGHT: A church functions like a human body, and all parts of the body work together to accomplish the purpose of the body.

Day 40

I AM JESUS—*A Reaching Body*

"And the church is His body, it is made full and complete by Christ,
who fills all things everywhere with Himself."
EPHESIANS 1:23, *NLT*

I am Jesus, the Church body. When you plant a new church, you put Me in that culture. When it is located in a culture different from your previous church, or even different from the way you live, I can reach the people of that culture. I love the people of every culture in the world. Remember, I commissioned you, "Go and make disciples of all the nations," i.e., *ethna* means people groups (Matthew 28:19, *NLT*). Because every person from every culture is lost in sin (Rom. 3:23; 5:12), I want My church to be a soul-winning body in every culture. Because We, the Trinity, love every individual in every culture, I want you to be a loving church body to witness to them (Acts 1:8). Because I will save everyone in every people group in the world, I want you to be an inviting church body.

Lord, I know You created all the cultures of the world, and You died for everyone in every culture; give me a burden to pray for them to be saved. Give me a vision of praying for a church body—Your presence—to be planted in every culture. Amen.

I am Jesus, the living body that preaches the gospel to all. I want you to plant Me in every language group in the world. You cannot do it by yourself, but you and all My other followers can do it together. Come together, pray together, plan together, give money together, and help preach the gospel to every people group in the world: "And the Good News about the Kingdom will be preached throughout the whole world, so that all nations will hear it; and then the end will come" (Matt. 24:14, *NLT*).

Lord Jesus, I know You are the church and I am in You. Wake me up to my responsibility to get the gospel to every person in every culture in the world. I will pray, work, give money, and do my part. Help me. Amen.

READING: Matt. 28:16-20; 1 Thess. 1:1-10

KEY THOUGHT: The church is the body of Jesus and He must be planted in every culture of the world to live in that group of people to win them to salvation.

I AM JESUS— *Persecution Makes Me Execptional*

"Saul was going everywhere to destroy the church . . . house to house . . . to throw them into prison."

ACTS 8:3, *NLT*

"Saul! Saul! Why are you persecuting me . . . I am Jesus, the one you are persecuting!"

ACTS 9:4-5, *NLT*

When anyone attacks believers for their faith, they are attacking Me, the Lord Jesus, who is the Church. Did you see that truth in today's scripture? Saul was persecuting believers, going house to house to arrest and put them in prison. But it wasn't just people he was persecuting; he was attacking Me. Remember, I indwell every believer. So to harm a believer for their faith is to harm Me. When someone attacks your faith, don't get angry and don't get even. Pray for your critics as Stephen did when he was executed by stoning for his faith: "Lord, lay not this sin to their charge" (Acts 7:60, *NLT*). Then demonstrate your victorious Christian attitude (1 John 4:4). Also, your prayers may lead some to salvation.

Lord, forgive me when I have sinned by criticizing my church, or any church. I now pray for my church: protect it, use it, and make it strong against attacks. I pray the same for my faith: make me strong in the face of criticism or attacks. May I have a forgiving spirit. Amen.

When someone criticizes or attacks your church, they attack Me. Yes, I will forgive them when they repent, but you should never stoop to their level by dishing out to them what they dish out to you. I said, "Bless those who curse you. Pray for those who hurt you" (Luke 6:28, *NLT*). You may eventually get them to follow Me. Remember, Stephen prayed for his persecutor—Saul—and Saul was saved to become Paul, My greatest apostle to the Gentiles.

Lord, work on my attitude to make me sweet, and give me faith to believe You will convert my persecutors to salvation. Amen.

READING: Acts 7:50–8:4; 9:1-19

KEY THOUGHT: When anyone persecutes the church, they are attacking Jesus. The positive response of believers to persecution can lead to the salvation of the attackers.

I AM JESUS—*Living in My Church*

"For where two or three gather together as my followers, I am there among them."
MATTHEW 18:20, *NLT*

I am Jesus the Church, the true assembly of believers. My followers believe I am the Son of God and Son of man, i.e., the God-man who was born of a virgin, lived without sin, and died on a cross for their sins (John 1:29). Those in a local church body have committed themselves to follow Me (Mark 1:11-12). When they all come together, they enjoy My presence because I said, "Where two or three are gathered together in My name, I am there in the midst of them" (Matt. 18:20, *NKJV*). Some people may just attend your assembly or may even join your assembly. But if they don't believe in Me for salvation, they are not My followers. They are not part of the body of Christ (Eph. 1:22-23). An authentic body of Christ is not a building, organization or religious service held on Sundays. The authentic body of Christ is Me, and if you believe in Me, then you are in My universal body.

> *Lord, I have read about You in the Bible and believe You are who You say You are. You are my Savior. Thank You for giving me a hope to live with You in heaven forever. You are also my Lord; lead me today. Amen.*

I am Jesus, the body of Christ. When you criticize the church, you are complaining about Me. When you don't attend on Sunday, I miss your worship. When you don't give your time, or your tithe, or your talents in service, My body doesn't grow. Remember, your faith is expressed in a dedicated relationship with Me.

> *Lord, teach me to reverence Your church as I reverence you. I love You with all my heart, I will serve You with all my talents, and I yield the control of all my "stuff" to You. I love You. Amen.*

READING: Eph. 4:9-16

KEY THOUGHT: The church is Jesus; therefore, you should relate to your church as you would relate to Jesus.

WEEK SEVEN

I AM JESUS
Pictures of My Exponential Church

The church is a supernatural creation by God the Father who sent Me, His Son, to die for the sins of the world. I died on the cross for the sins of lost people. Now those who are saved are in My body—Jesus, the local church—to live for Me in the world. The night before I died, I promised, "You in Me, and I in you" (John 14:20, *NKJV*). All Christians were placed into Me on the cross and now I live in them. But the picture analogy continues; today a believer is a member of My local church body. At the same time I am in the believer, ministering to the lost world through them in My church.

Day 43

I AM JESUS—*The Church's Many Pictures*

"So now you Gentiles are no longer strangers and foreigners. You are citizens along with all of God's holy people. You are members of God's family. Together, we are his house, built on the foundation of the apostles and the prophets. And the cornerstone is Christ Jesus himself. We are carefully joined together in him, becoming a holy temple for the Lord. Through him you Gentiles are also being made part of this dwelling where God lives by his Spirit."

EPHESIANS 2:19-22, *NLT*

I am Jesus, the Church (Eph. 1:22-23). But did you see My other church names in today's reading? I am called "the household of God," so everyone in My house is family; you are called a child of God. Notice, you are no longer strangers or foreigners, but a fellow citizen and a member of the family. My church is also called a *Temple*, and I am the cornerstone of that sanctuary. When I come into your life at salvation (Eph. 3:17), you also were placed into Me. Paul frequently calls this "in Christ." "At that day you will know that . . . you (are) in Me, and I in you" (John 14:20, *NKJV*). So, the church is a household; and you are in Me.

Lord, I love my church because I love You. I come seeking Your presence when I worship. But more than that, I want Your presence with me 24/7. Amen.

Don't think of your church as an organization, or meetings with programs. I am the Church, and today's reading says it is "this dwelling where God lives" (Eph. 2:22, *NLT*). The church is My body and My life. Next, it is the dwelling place of the Father, and His majesty and glory live there. Then the Holy Spirit indwells the church (1 Cor. 3:16). My church has met in caves, in mountains, and catacombs under the city of Rome. My church has met in tents, under the open sky, and in some of the most beautiful structures in the world. But those were only outward buildings. The church meets where My presence dwells.

Lord, I will go to church to meet You. It is not about friends or a position where I serve, and it's not about habit. It's all about You. Since You indwell me, I will live in Your church. Amen.

READING: Eph. 2:14-22; 1 Cor. 3:9-23

KEY THOUGHT: The church has many names; today's lesson pictures Jesus as the dwelling place where the church assembles.

I AM JESUS—*My Church the Bride*

"The bride, the Lamb's wife."
DEUTERONOMY 21:9, *NKJV*

"You as a pure bride to one husband—Christ."
2 CORINTHIANS 11:2, *NLT*

The church is pictured as My bride. A bride is beautiful to the groom; all those who are saved are beautiful to Me because I first loved them. Just as a bride gives herself to her husband, so to you must give yourself to Me. You will do that because you love Me. It will be easy to love Me when you realize how much I love you. How much is that? I gave Myself in death to forgive your sins. The key ingredient in a marriage relationship is love. Keep our relationship open, growing, and warm. Love is the greatest quality in life. Love me as I love you.

Lord, forgive me when I sin against You and Your love. Cleanse me and restore me to intimate fellowship. I want to serve You because I love You and because You love me. You have given me eternal life and everlasting fellowship. Make me worthy of Your love. Amen.

Just as a bride must be pure for her husband, so to I want you to be holy, separated from sin to Me. Just as a bride lives with her husband, you will live forever with Me. Just as a bride forsakes all others for her husband, turn your back on all religions, and all the gods of all religions. I am Jesus, the Son of God; I am your only way to the heavenly Father (John 14:6).

Lord, I give myself completely to You from this day forward to do everything You want me to do. Because we are one (John 14:20), I will follow You, serve You and love You. Amen.

READING: Rev. 19:7-10; Eph. 5:23-32

KEY THOUGHT: The Bible describes the church as a bride, so the church must relate to Christ just as a bride relates to her husband.

I AM JESUS—*Shepherd of My Flock*

"Guard yourselves and God's people. Feed and shepherd God's flock—his church, purchased with his own blood . . . I know that false teachers, like vicious wolves, will come in . . . not sparing the flock."

ACTS 20:28-29, NLT

My church is like a flock of sheep that needs human shepherds—pastors—to tend to them. I am the Chief Shepherd (1 Pet. 5:4), and My pastors are under-shepherds. A flock needs three things: (1) tending or leading, because sheep cannot lead themselves, (2) feeding, a shepherd finds green pastures, and (3) protection, a flock must be guarded from false teachers who will lead them astray and from diseases like sin that will destroy them. I am Jesus, your Shepherd; stay close to Me, so I can lead, feed, and protect you.

Lord, You are my Shepherd, I will lay down in Your green pastures, lead me beside still cool spiritual waters to restore my soul. Protect me when I walk through the valley of the shadow of death (Ps. 23:1-4). Amen.

You are My church, the flock for whom I gave Myself (John 10:11). As an earthly shepherd loves his sheep, so I love you and all others in your church. Because of that, I am the Shepherd who goes out in the storm to find lost sheep in the wilderness (Luke 15:3-7). One day I will return from heaven to take you and every one of My sheep to live with Me forever: "When the Chief Shepherd appears, you will receive the crown of glory" (1 Pet. 5:4).

Lord, You prepare a table of food to feed me, and You anoint my head and bruises with oil, and You give me a cup that is filled to the brim. Thank You for being my Shepherd (Ps. 23:4-6). Amen.

READING: Ps. 23:1-6; John 10:1-18

KEY THOUGHT: My church is called a flock and My believers are called sheep. I will look after them like the Shepherd of Psalm 23.

Day 46

I AM JESUS—*A Church Garden*

"I [Paul] planted the seed in your hearts, and Apollos watered it, but it was God who made it grow . . . the one who plants and the one who waters work together . . . for we are both God's workers. And you are God's field."

1 CORINTHIANS 3:6, 8-9, *NLT*

I am Jesus the church, which is described as a garden. The focus is individuals growing in Christian faith and inner character. But also the church body is growing in attendance, evangelistic outreach, numbers and love. The church is shown as a field or trees (Israel is an olive or fig tree and the church is a vine), or a farm to produce a harvest of fruit or the beauty of flowers. The church is a cultivated plot of ground where weeds and rocks are removed, seed is sown, and plants are cared for until the harvest. What do these pictures tell you? You must depend on Me alone as the source of life, growth and harvest. I said, "Abide in Me, and I in you. As the branch cannot bear fruit of itself, unless it abides in the vine, neither can you, unless you abide in Me" (John 15:4, *NKJV*).

Lord, help me grow to produce fruit for Your glory. I am different from all other seeds in the church garden. Help Me produce fruit both in character growth and winning the lost. I want my fruit to satisfy hungry and needy people. Amen.

Did you see that double transference? "You abide in Me and I abide in you." At salvation I enter your heart to give you eternal life. Then you must abide in Me to keep growing and producing fruit. You abide in Me by prayer, obeying My words in Scripture, serving and ministering to others. But most of all by intimate fellowship and worship. Don't get cut off from Me like a withered-up branch lying on the ground.

Lord, I will abide in You so Your life-giving energy can flow into my life. It is peaceful when I am close to You, letting fruit grow in my life. I want to get closer to You to produce more fruit. Amen.

READING: 1 Cor. 3:5-9; John 15:1-8

KEY THOUGHT: My church is like a garden where plants (people) grow to produce fruit.

I AM JESUS—*A Growing Temple*

"I [Paul] have laid the foundation . . . now others are building it.
No one can lay any foundation other than—Jesus Christ . . . all of you together are
the temple of God and that the Spirit of God lives in you."

1 CORINTHIANS 3:10-11, 16, *NLT*

I am Jesus, a living temple. Each of you is a part of the construction material. Some are gold, silver, jewels, wood, hay and stubble. When you get to heaven it will be revealed what kind of construction stone you are (3:13). Some will be rewarded; others will have their works burned up (3:14-15). So strive to be pure, diligent and worthy, because you are My temple, and I want you and My church to be holy.

Lord, thank You for making me a part of Your church—you body. Forgive any
and all of my sin; cleanse me. I will live a holy life to please You and serve You.
Amen.

I build a temple to dwell in. After all the workers finished Solomon's Temple, it was beautiful, gold plated, and magnificent to the eye. But its real beauty was when the Father, I and the Holy Spirit indwelt it: "A thick cloud filled the temple . . . the glorious presence of the Lord filled the Temple of God" (2 Chron. 5:13-14, *NLT*). Let Me fill your life; you will be a beautiful temple and people will see My presence in your life.

Lord, come dwell in my life. Fill my mind with Your presence.
Quiet my emotions to love and worship You, bend my will to serve You.
Come make Your home in my heart. Amen.

READING: 1 Cor. 3:10-17; 2 Chron. 5:1-14

KEY THOUGHT: My church is a temple where I live. Build it to be beautiful and functional, because I will come indwell it.

I AM JESUS—*A Church of Priests*

"You are a chosen generation, a royal priesthood, a holy people . . .
show the praises to Him who called you."
1 PETER 2:9, *NKJV*

"Let us continually offer the sacrifice of praise to God, that is, the fruit of our lips."
HEBREWS 13:15, *NKJV*

My Old Testament priest offered the sacrifice of blood to Me as a symbol of cleansing and forgiveness. But I am the Priest who offered My blood for the world (1 Tim. 2:5). Now My church is made up of priests—every believer—who offer the sacrifices of worship and praise. Have you done that today? Because I—your High Priest—saved your soul, you should continually offer praise and worship to God the Father.

Lord I come to You—my High Priest—thanking You for my salvation, and for
complete cleansing from all sin (1 John 1:9). Now I offer praises and worship for
Your extraordinary gift of salvation. Amen.

You are a priest. You should pray daily for yourself, conferring your sin (1 John 1:4), and seeking to grow spiritually. Second, you should intercede for believers, rulers, and My workers to carry out the Great Commission around the world (1 Tim. 2:1). Then you should worship and praise the Father, Holy Spirit and Me in worship.

Lord, I ask forgiveness for my failure to be your priest, doing what You require.
I pray for all people everywhere (1 Tim. 2:1-5). Next, I intercede for the salvation
of lost family and friends. Finally I offer You worship—the sacrifice of my lips and
words. Be glorified in me, in my church and the world. Amen.

READING: I Pet. 2:1-15; 1 Tim. 2:1-8

KEY THOUGHT: My church is a priesthood, and each member is a priest who intercedes and offers worship to the Father.

I AM JESUS—*A Church of People Different*

*"The human body has many parts, but the many parts make up one whole body.
So it is with the body of Christ."*

1 CORINTHIANS 12:12, *NLT*

"Bodies have many parts and God has put each part just where He wants it."

1 CORINTHIANS 12:19, *NLT*

My church is called a body, which is made up of lots of different people—men, women and children. But each person is part of the body, just like your body has arms, eyes, feet, etc. Just as each part of your physical body must work in harmony with the whole, every believer must work in harmony with all others. Can you sing, speak, counsel, or give lots of money? Serve your church body where you are strongest and can do the most good. Can you pray, serve, or teach? I want every believer in My church to sacrifice and work hard; let's change the world!

*Lord, I am not the best in my church. Some people sing better than me,
whereas I can sing better than a few others. Use me—use all of us—to glorify You
in music. I don't want to be in competition with others; I want to
cooperate with them. Amen.*

My body is different in various cultures. Some churches are in the jungle, others in suburbia, and still others in skyscrapers in metropolitan areas. Different churches reach different kinds of people. Some of My churches are strong in teaching, while others are strong in worship—exaltation—and still others have practical preaching. And then some churches meet in small groups like underground churches. Find out your strength and use it for your church to reach lost people. Find out the strength of your church and support its outreach. Let's change the world.

*Lord, thank You for my church, for the way they worship and serve and care for
one another. May I care for them as much as You care for them. Amen.*

READING: 1 Cor. 12:1-31

KEY THOUGHT: The church is a unified body, yet its members are different in age, talent, background, training, and spiritual gifts. All must work together to carry out the Great Commission.

Your 50th Day of Prayer

I have talked to you in 7 weekly devotionals, telling you how My church will change the world. Now we come to the 50th devotional. It is all about the end—the Great Commission is completed. This lesson is about the Omegan—the one person somewhere on Earth who will hear the gospel (could be man, woman or child) and will accept salvation. Omega means the last, as alpha means the first. When the last person is saved, immediately the Father will send Me to go gather My church—living and dead—the Great Commission is completed. At least one person from every *ethne* tribe has become a follower of Me. What will you do to reach the Omegan? I know that Elmer Towns prays daily that one of his students will reach the Omegan for salvation.

Day 50

I AM JESUS—*Looking for Omegan*

"And the Good News about the Kingdom will be preached throughout the whole world, so that all nations will hear it; and then the end will come."

MATTHEW 24:14, *NLT*

I am Jesus who gave you the Great Commission to evangelize every tribe on Earth. You are to witness as effectively as possible, to as many people as possible, for as long as possible. When will the task be finished, and when will you be done? The answer is simple. When the gospel has been preached in every people group (Gk. *ethne* or culture). Some have called the last person to be saved Omegan. This name comes from the Greek alphabet, beginning with the letter Alpha and ending with Omega. When the last person believes for salvation, the Father will say to Me, "Go get Our people and bring them home." Then I will come to rapture all My followers to heaven. The dead in Christ will be caught up first (1 Thess. 4:16). Then those who are alive will instantly follow them to heaven (1 Thess. 4:17).

Lord, I am ready for Your return. I am saved and ready to go.
But I have unsaved friends and family. Help me reach them with the message
before it is too late. I pray for their salvation. Amen.

I am Jesus who will transform your bodies and I will take you to heaven. Just as you were transformed inwardly when you were saved, you will then have a new body as I rapture you to be with Me. Your old sinful nature in the future will be gone. You will know Me and all others as you are known (1 John 3:2). You will join the massive worshiping choir before the throne, singing, "You are worthy, O Lord our God, to receive glory and honor and power" (Rev. 4:11, *NLT*).

Lord, I look forward to that instant when You transform me into a likeness like
Yourself. But while I am on the earth, use me to win lost people to You.
I will work because of the Day of Your coming. Amen.

READING: Matt. 24:1-14; Rev. 4:1-11

KEY THOUGHT: The Great Commission will be finished when the gospel is preached to the last culture (*ethne*) and the last person is saved.